St. Andrew's Convent
1975

Enthusiasm in the Spirit

Enthusiasm in the Spirit

Robert Wild
Priest of Madonna House

AVE MARIA PRESS
Notre Dame, Indiana 46556

Library of Congress Catalog Card Number: 75-14742

International Standard Book Number: 0-87793-102-X (paper)
0-87793-101-1 (cloth)

Printed in the United States of America

Cover Design: Carolyn Desch

To my parents, Henry and Lillian Wild . . .

for every conceivable reason.

But to return to St. Anthony. Did I see him before me, I might be tempted, with my cut and dried opinions, and my matter-of-fact ways, and my selfishness and pusillanimity, to consider him somewhat of an enthusiast; but what I desire to point out to the reader . . . is the subdued and Christian form which was taken by his enthusiasm, if it must be so called. It was not vulgar, bustling, imbecile, unstable, undutiful; it was calm and composed, manly, intrepid, magnanimous, full of affectionate loyalty to the Church and to the truth.

John Henry Cardinal Newman,
"Anthony in Conflict" in
Essays and Sketches

Contents

Introduction

"Charismatic renewal" is a very elusive phrase. It is elusive because its meaning is a relational one, dependent on the state of the person when he or she came into contact with the renewal. It differs from Pentecostalism as a denomination. When a Pentecostal minister preaches, he is not preaching the charismatic renewal. He is preaching the gospel as understood in his tradition of Pentecostalism. For him it is the whole gospel, pure and simple. Similarly, when a Lutheran or a Roman Catholic missionary goes to a foreign land, both preach the gospel as best they can in the light of their own particular tradition. They do not intend to leave anything of the gospel out.

On the other hand, charismatic renewal implies a reality which is being renewed. It implies that there already exists some sort of faith foundation, more or less complete, which is being renewed, deepened, or expanded. In relation to the individual, charismatic renewal can mean a variety of different things. Many people in our churches are only nominal Christians. It may very well be that when they come into contact with the charismatic renewal it spells the difference between Christ and no Christ, light and darkness. Or perhaps they have never heard of the Holy Spirit and his gifts even though they have been "Christians" all their lives. For them, indeed, the charismatic renewal is more than a renewal. It might very well be the gospel itself. But it is only such because of a defective Christian formation.

If this is so, if the charismatic renewal actually does admit of a variety of meanings in the lives of people, how come to any kind of definition?

It is possible to set up a theoretical model of relation. For the sake of clarification, we can define the poles of the relation, and then allow individuals to make their own personal adjustments. It is possible to get a rather definite picture of the charismatic renewal as a movement. A movement has certain teachings, a literature, seminar topics at conventions, and so forth. One might say that this is the objective aspect of the renewal.

As the theoretical subject meeting this renewal, we will postulate a person in the Roman Catholic communion who has a fairly firm grasp, in both theory and daily living, of the essentials of his faith. From this standpoint, the charismatic renewal does not offer any new doctrine. On the other hand, since it is a renewal, it is capable of bringing a deepening to many aspects of our Church life. It is one of the purposes of this book to explore some aspects of this charismatic renewal in Roman Catholic theology and practice.

If the charismatic renewal is seen as a movement merging with an already existent understanding and living of the essential gospel message, one way to view it is in the context of a *spirituality*. A spirituality is a particular way of conceiving and realizing the Christian life. It is a matter of emphasis, of focus, of stressing certain doctrines and expressions instead of others. Love, the goal of the Christian life, can be deepened in a variety of ways.

Throughout the history of the Church, Christendom has been renewed by the Holy Spirit in just such a variety of ways. We could even say that the Church has been charismatically renewed before, but the charisms of the Spirit took on different forms.

In the third century, when Anthony heard the call of Christ, he headed for the deepest part of the desert. Anthony had been a Christian for many years, but one day he was renewed. Why did he go into solitude, and thus begin a movement which many thousands personally followed, and whose lives inspired many more thousands to deeper lives in the Lord? The only answer is that it was a gift of the Spirit. Their prayer life was renewed, not by coming together for prayer meetings, but just the opposite, by getting as far away from each other as possible! And, yet, prayer was renewed. The flight into the desert was a spirituality, a movement of the Spirit which was appropriate for the times and a wellspring of deep renewal in the Church.

In the sixth century, Benedict also heard the call of the Lord in a powerful way. Eventually he was led, not into the desert, but into forming communities of people who lived together in the spirit of the gospel. They didn't get together for spontaneous prayer meetings either, but the Spirit did renew their prayer. The form it took was the elaboration of the Divine Office in choir, a form of prayer that was appropriate and meaningful for them. If it be asked why Benedict formed communities instead of living

alone in the desert, the answer again can only be the movement of the Spirit. It was a particular spirituality of the
time.

In the 12th century another man, Francis, also heard
the call of Christ. His spirituality was neither to stay in
the desert nor to take a vow of stability in a closed community. He modified both of these forms by spending time
in solitude *and* community. But his basic thrust was to
wander freely among the people and preach the gospel.
Thus arose the mendicant orders with their strong emphasis
on poverty and reaching the people with the message of
Christ. Why did he bring the religious life out of the en-
closures like this? The same answer as before: a gift of
the Spirit. The Franciscan spirituality was a spirituality
for the times, and it renewed the life of the Church.

Having said this, perhaps it is not too important what
label we put on the charismatic renewal, whether a spirituality, a renewal, a movement, or a phenomenon of the
Spirit. Labels have a tendency to divide people into different camps, people who often basically agree on what is
happening but who call it by different names for different
reasons. Actually, the term "spirituality" is a rather recent
word in the history of the Church. After the dissolution of
religious orders in France, and then in the aftermath of
restoration, orders attempted to regain their distinctive "spiritualities." Many of the distinctions made then were somewhat arbitrary and artificial. It seemed as if each order
was trying to nurture and protect and define its own spirituality so as to distinguish itself from others. In the attempt, it must be admitted that some of these distinctions
were mere words.

Everyone will agree that what we are concerned about
is the spirituality of the gospel. Many currents in the

Church are tending to forge one spirituality, the spirituality of the gospel. It may also be true that the charismatic renewal does not fit any of our present categories; it is my belief, however, that a good case could be made for its being a spirituality. This latter concept would need further clarification, more than present space allows. Again, the labels are not too important.

What is important is some of the theological principles involved. It is important that we do not impose spiritual straitjackets on people who may be called to other expressions of their life in the Spirit. Let us, for example, consider briefly the spirituality of St. Therese of the Child Jesus, the Little Flower.

There is no record of her ever having spoken in tongues. In her Carmel there were no spontaneous prayer meetings. Neither is there much evidence of the gift of prophecy (as commonly expressed or understood in the present renewal). She does not seem to have gone around "witnessing" too much to her sisters, again, in the sense that term is used today. If she were alive today, I doubt if her life in the Lord would qualify as charismatic. And if we met her today, I think most would agree that she would not be considered as being involved in the charismatic renewal.

"Ah," you will say, "but she had the essence of the charismatic renewal. She was a great lover of Christ, and she undoubtedly had all the fruits of the Spirit which are the goal of the gifts."

Exactly—but I would not put it that way. I would not say that she had the essence of the charismatic renewal: She had the essence of the Christian life. That essence is attainable by many different routes and by many different paths.

I think there is a definite and real sense (which would have to be clearly defined) in which it is true to say that the charismatic renewal is optional. But—and this is a big "but"—*growth in the Spirit is not optional.* Growth in witnessing to Christ is *not optional.* Growth in prayer is *not optional.* Growth in being attuned to the manifestations of the Spirit in the world today is *not optional.* Deeper desire for the gifts that God wants to give us is *not optional.*

What must be safeguarded is the freedom of God's Spirit and the freedom of his children to respond to him. Theologically we must be convinced that the Spirit really can lead people to express all the above aspects of the Christian life in ways other than those manifested in the charismatic renewal.

On the other hand, people must not use this theological principle as an excuse for not exploring what the Spirit is doing in the charismatic renewal. I don't think I am contradicting myself. As will be mentioned in various ways throughout this book, the renewal has reached a stage of legitimacy (for want of a better word) in the churches. Everyone must seriously question his reasons for not trying to understand what the Spirit is saying to the churches in this movement.

After all, we pray and pray day after day, begging God to come to our aid, to help us, to send his Spirit, etc. All of us must tremble with a holy fear lest, because of our lack of generosity, *we rationalize away his action when he does come.* There are various ways to express our faith and to grow in the Spirit. *But,* one must really be convinced that he or she *is* being led by another way, and not just using this "other way" as an excuse for failing to explore what the Lord is doing in the renewal.

One of the general characteristics usually associated

with the charismatic renewal is enthusiasm (spontaneity, freedom) in the Spirit. Often in practice (if not in theory) this tendency is considered to be opposed to realities such as Church, institution and structure. Some people who become involved in the charismatic renewal still find it necessary to leave their churches for a freer life in the Spirit. Most often, such departures are due to a lack of understanding of their own tradition on the part of the enthusiasts, or to a lack of sympathy and assistance on the part of those in their churches who ought to help them understand this new freedom of the Spirit.

Enthusiasm without structure and channeling is meaningless and often destructive; structure without enthusiasm is sterile and lifeless. To quote again from the *Essays* of Cardinal Newman referred to at the beginning:

> It would not be consistent with our present argument to rescue him [Anthony] from the imputation of enthusiasm: he must be here considered as an enthusiast, else I cannot make use of him; the very drift of my account of him being to show how enthusiasm is sobered and refined by being submitted to the discipline of the Church, instead of being allowed to run wild externally to it.

In the same manner, I have no intention of rescuing those involved in the charismatic renewal from the imputation of enthusiasm. How desperately all the churches need enthusiasm! As a *Time* essay on the "Jesus Revolution" concluded: "Enthusiasm is not the only virtue, but God knows, apathy is none at all!" As Newman said of Anthony, could we also say that unless we are enthusiastic the Lord cannot make use of us either?

Enthusiasts are not often ill-willed people. They have seen a vision; they are convinced it is the one and only answer to life's meaning. Enthusiasm is a great and noble sentiment—thus all the greater tragedy when it is not guided in the right directions. Cardinal Newman puts these words in the mouth of the Church:

> My child, you may do as many great things as you will: but I have already made a list for you to select from. You are too docile to pursue ends merely because they are of your own choosing; you seek them because they are *great*. You wish to live above the common course of a Christian: I can teach you to do this, yet without arrogance.

What a tragedy if people with enthusiasm for Christ leave the churches. The churches need enthusiasm so badly. This book is written especially to help Catholics channel their enthusiasm in the right directions. It is written with a threefold conviction: 1) that the charismatic renewal is a Spirit-inspired spirituality for our times; 2) that it needs constantly to be critically examined; and 3) that people in the institutional churches, in our case the Roman Catholic Church, need help in understanding and integrating this work of the Spirit into their traditional Church devotion and practice. This is not meant to be an introductory book. Most of the chapters presuppose acquaintance with the basic literature concerning the charismatic renewal.

Cardinal Newman sensed that Anthony, for all his seeking after solitude and silence, was an enthusiast, a charismatic person at heart. Anthony, in this sense, exemplifies one of the main contentions of this book—that the

Spirit's renewal of hearts, and thus his charisms, can take on a variety of forms. The charismatic renewal of today is one such form, one way of many in the history of the Church—and always a gift.

Special thanks to Sister Florette Amyot of the Prayer House of Peace in Combermere who read the entire manuscript and offered many helpful suggestions.

Madonna House
Combermere, Ontario

Chapter 1

Not a Spirit of Fear

— *2 Tm 1:7*

Though there are more than enough books to introduce Catholics to the charismatic renewal, this first chapter
is, in a sense, addressed to those who have not yet got up
the courage to get their feet wet. I believe the charismatic
renewal is part of the Spirit's ongoing renewal of hearts. It
is not, of course, a matter of banding together with "charismatic people" and attending "charismatic conferences" and
reading "charismatic books," although this might be a good
place to begin. Rather, it is a matter of believing in and
desiring to have operative in one's life the gifts of the Spirit
which are being renewed among God's people today in a
marvelous way.

There are still too many people who have heard about
the charismatic renewal but who are afraid of getting involved in it. They wish to study it and observe it from the
outside before committing themselves. I would hope to
show that in our life with God, such detached insight is not
possible. G. K. Chesterton said that, from the outside, the
Catholic Church appeared cold and forbidding, like a huge
stone cathedral. It was only after he stuck his head through
the window that he began to understand the warmth of the
interior. The charismatic renewal is a "conversion move-

ment" in the Christian body today. No one likes to be converted continually. Once or twice at the beginning of our lives was enough!

As is well known, the Greek word for conversion, *metanoia,* has something to do with making a decision concerning various paths open to us. We are aware in our consciousness of more elevated options, the call of the Spirit to grow. Failure to respond is our lack of conversion, and we label this selfishness, lack of love and lack of faith. This failure to respond is all that and more. Here we wish to consider this lack of conversion as a lack of *courage,* and to show how this defect is close to the heart of the matter.

While I am gently implying here that such lack of courage may be the reason why some people have not investigated the charismatic renewal more closely, the point of this chapter applies to every call of the Spirit. We ought to presuppose that there are many other aspects to the total act of conversion, such as the ability to listen to the Spirit and a general knowledge of the direction in which to move. But we start our analysis at the point where we realize our call to "come up higher," and we stand at the threshold, hesitating. This hesitation will be experienced before one gets involved in the charismatic renewal, and at almost every step along the way. The exercise of each of the gifts demands a certain amount of courage and stepping out in faith.

One reason for such hesitation is that we cannot see *clearly* where we are going. A fruitful topic for meditation here is what several schools of modern philosophy are saying about action and the nature of truth. We think it possible to be able to know about a situation and analyze it *before* we enter into it. We want to be completely sure, at ease, and safe about where we are headed.

For much of modern philosophy, the truth about human existence is available only *consequent to action*. This was a cardinal point in the writings of the French philosopher Maurice Blondel: "For Blondel, the faculty of the real is not the intellect but man's involvement in the whole of life. For Blondel, action is the organ of truth. The word 'action' as used by the French philosopher refers to man's willing, choosing and doing, understood as the profound and many-leveled self-affirmation by which he becomes himself . . . ."[1]

Since living is prior to our reflection about it (the stance of the phenomenologist), one principle of growth for us, one element in all attempts at conversion, should be the realization of the uselessness of fearing to enter a new situation because of its unfamiliarity. It is precisely *by entering* that its mysteries will be revealed to us.

The same notion is to be found in Paul Tillich's brilliant book, *The Courage to Be,* where he says that "courage can show us what being is."[2] By this he means (as is evident throughout the book) that it is only by the act of the will implied by courage that reality is illuminated. Before the act of courage our anxieties and fears cloak everything with unnameable masks:

> If we strip them [fears] of these masks their own countenance appears and the fear they produce disappears. This is true even of death. Since every day a little of our life is taken from us—since we are dying every day—the final hour when we cease to exist does not of itself bring death; it merely completes the process. The horrors connected with it are a matter of imagination.[3]

Existentialism certainly does not have all the *answers,* but it has helped us to see more clearly that each person must take on the responsibility *to be,* and that what this means is only gradually revealed to us: "Existential analysis can do nothing more than make it clear to me that I can understand love only by loving. No analysis can take the place of my duty to understand my love as an encounter in my own personal existence."[4] Bultmann says it "can do nothing more" because existentialism does not "furnish us an ideal pattern of existence."[5] Existentialists are very good in describing for us our anxieties when faced with the facts of life, but they do not tell us what to choose. They do not offer us any positive program for life, but remind us very forcibly that we can live no one's life but our own.

Prior, then, to our own actual loving and believing, there can be no adequate understanding of just how the next step will determine our self-image, or our relationship to God and to others. At the deepest level, perhaps it is precisely this "redefining" of ourselves that we fear.

We know who we are now, confused as this picture may be. We have such and such limits ("define" means to set limits) to our self-concept, and because of this image and the way we act, the responses of others toward us are also defined. We are comfortable here. We feel at home with this confused image. We would certainly like to acquire more knowledge about ourselves—but without actually taking any risks, without actually acting! But this is precisely what is not possible. We cannot know beforehand what the taking of the next step will do to us as far as our "self-image" is concerned. It is only in the taking of the next step that reality, and the reality about ourselves, will be disclosed to us.

A brief meditation on this process may help here. We

have all had to enter, at one time or another, a dark room or building which we had never been in before. We did not know what was inside, nor our way around. For some reason (probably necessity) we went in. At first we were a bit afraid as we fumbled around for the light switch. We turned the light on and gradually became comfortable.

The steps we are asked to take on the road to deeper life are analogous to this situation. We are continually summoned, as it were, to enter dark rooms. At first we refuse because we do not know what is in there. Finally, we take the plunge. We enter. After a while, understanding occurs, we become acclimated to a new self-image and become more comfortable in a new consciousness.

What we are involved in, however, is a never-ending process. Always, at the other end of that room, is another door, and the whole interior dynamic repeats itself.

Each of us, at the present time, is settled down in a particular room. If we are not directly looking at it, we are nevertheless aware of another door at the far end of our room. We are all trying to get up enough courage to open that door. If we do not open it, the best we can do is walk around in circles in our little room. (All our rooms are very small compared to what the Lord has in store for us.)

We often call this walking around in circles "growing more mature." Actually, in our more honest moments, we know we are simply biding our time. We know that we are not exploring new rooms but only neurotically making a big thing out of the same old room. We are repeating a routine form of existence. In short, we are in a rut. It's the door at the other end of the room that bothers us. The only way out of the room is courage.

It is a tragedy that we forget so quickly our past

experience of the light going on. To keep advancing into new rooms we need to build on our past and have confidence that if the light has gone on before it will go on again. It is also helpful to realize that our human existence is constituted again and again by a leaving of the old and familiar and entering into the new and unfamiliar.

We were pulled, screaming, from the warmth and security of the womb into the unknown world beyond. We rebelled, but soon settled down in our mother's arms and then in the security of the family. Another day came. There were rumblings about "going to school" and how we will just love meeting all the new girls and boys! We were pushed again from the security of the home into the still larger world of school and new people. We probably cannot remember now, but the leaving of each class to advance into the next grade was a little bit of a traumatic experience. Then high school, college, a job, ties with home and familiar people constantly broken and replaced. Old friends move, and we move, and on and on.

When will we understand that we are involved in a continual process of continually moving into wider and wider worlds? One day we will have to leave whatever security we have tried to amass during our lifetime and pass over into the world beyond death. Passing into new worlds is part of life. We are all afraid of leaving the familiar behind. There should come a time in our lives, however, when we assimilate this process, recognize there is no escaping it, and consciously enter into it by courageously coming to terms with it. Perhaps much pain in life is due to the resistance we offer to this inevitable dynamic of growth. We should facilitate it and not resist it.

Incidentally, this same lack of courage may be a key factor in the difficulties we experience with self-denial in general. It is a curious fact that in other circumstances and for other reasons, we can suffer a great deal of physical hardship. The gruelling spring training of athletes, the real emotional and physical pain involved in learning how to ski or simply play the piano, the energy to fight sleep all night during a party or watching three late movies—to mention only a few. But let us attempt to do a little fasting, or spend a few hours during the night in prayer, or sleep on the floor, and we simply cannot do it. We are not that strong!

What's the difference? The difference is that in the former cases, the pain is not so directly related to the journey to God, although it could be. In the latter instances, we are on a bit more shaky ground (actually more solid, if only we believed). We are abandoning more of our security. There is the lurking fear that without these material things our security will be undermined.

Part of every act of true self-denial must be courage, the courage to abandon the security of material things and to actually experience their loss. This is the only way we can experience as well the power of God upholding us. What we fear is that when we try to lean on God, we will fall over, that no one will be there. The only way to find out is to lean!

Faith, in this context, means to trust in some security when no security can be seen. It is, as Luther once said, "the readiness to enter confidently into the darkness of the future. For in the world, nothing of God and his action is visible or can be visible to men who seek security in the world."[6] By "world" here we could understand "everything in which we seek security which is not God." God becomes visible only when we lean on him. Thus the actual realization of being upheld by God cannot be a mere abstraction or analyzed or "believed in" beforehand as a "truth of the spiritual life." It has to be experienced. Courage is the only door to that experience.

This power to act courageously against all the fears and anxieties within and about us is ultimately grounded in the reality of God. "Do not be afraid, for I am with you; stop being anxious and watchful, for I am your God. I am holding you by the right hand; I tell you, 'Do not be afraid,' I will help you" (Is 41: 10, 13). It is "the courage of confidence in the personal reality which is encountered in the religious experience."[7] Thus, this courage must be an element in every true act of faith. In fact, Tillich wrote his book precisely as an interpretation of faith through an analysis of courage "because I believe that 'faith' needs such a reinterpretation more than any other religious term."[8]

It is now a truism that faith, in the sense of trust, is the most essential virtue of the bible. It is a confidence in the power of God to save and thus to heal. Faith, for Tillich, is this state of being grasped by this gracious power of Being Itself. It is in this kind of faith that courage is born. Faith which lacks this dimension of courage is sterile. A faith which says that it believes that God exists and cares, and on the other hand lacks courage to enter more deeply into relationship with God—such a faith has much to be desired. Conversion, then, understood as the continual process or growth to which we are called, demands courage as an essential ingredient.

Up to this point our description may have sounded a bit grim, what with going into dark rooms and everything. It wasn't meant to be. We are not speaking of a "grit your teeth and plunge in" type of courage, although a certain amount of fear is compatible with courage. We are speaking about a type of courage which, though accompanied by fear, is nevertheless confident, strong, realizing that all passovers have their pain, but are necessary for new life.

Even besides this strength and confidence, there is still another element which would put the crowning feature on our courage. It is the spirit of adventure.

Adventure is a frequent theme in the writings of the American process theologians. Their philosophical parent, Alfred N. Whitehead, has written: "A race preserves its vigor so long as it harbors a real contrast between what has been and what may be; so long as it is nerved by the vigor to adventure beyond the safeties of the past. Without adventure civilization is in decay."[9]

The same idea could and does apply to individuals. We would like to do away with the contrast which is always before us of what we are and what we could be—the contrast between the room we are in and the door at the other end. We look upon that door as a threat to our security rather than as the gateway to high adventure of the spirit. We would like to do away with the awareness of that door, failing to realize that it is this tension, this vigor, which is the deepest sign of life in us.

In another place Whitehead says: "Even perfection will not bear the tedium of indefinite repetitions. Adventure . . . namely the search for new perfections, is necessary."[10] This continued striving toward new perfections "gives a thrill keener than any prolonged halt in a stage of attainment with the major variations completely tried out."[11] Cultures and individuals decline when life merely repeats itself by a constant reproduction of past successes. "It's the same routine" is the price we pay for the lack of courage to open new doors. As Baum says, "one thing the Good News means is that tomorrow *can be* different from today."[12] It *can be* different if we will do what the Lord told us to do, trust him—trust him by actually leaning on him, which takes courage.

Process theologians see God as the one who constantly offers new options and possibilities for growth. God is the one who is constantly presenting us with new ideals and new visions of growth. "God is the urge toward adventure and the ground of the possibility of the response."[13] God is constantly summoning us to wider worlds. The passage from nothingness to existence was a long journey indeed, happening without our efforts. The journey into new worlds ahead of us requires our courage and trust in him who brought us over the first immense gulf. How long will it take us before we discover that it is the Lord behind every door? (Rv 3:20).

The charismatic renewal just may be one of the doors the Lord is asking Christians of our day to open. I believe it is. Again, not necessarily in the sense of joining and associating with "charismatic groups," but in the sense of living by the Spirit and having the gifts of the Holy Spirit at work in their lives. What do we have to lose? Who knows, it may be the beginning of the greatest adventure of your life!

Chapter 2

The Holy Spirit Fell on Them

— Acts 11:15

It is important at the very outset of our study to realize that what is happening in the charismatic renewal has excellent scriptural foundations. The best of modern scholarship confirms the fact that the early Christians' consciousness was shot through with a new awareness of the Spirit's presence, and with vivid experiences of his power at work among them through his gifts. I would like to outline, in this chapter, the testimony of the New Testament in regard to the experience of the Holy Spirit. Many of the topics treated then in subsequent chapters can be seen in a better scriptural perspective.

But before going on to consider this biblical testimony, there is one very important point to make which is vital to Catholics' theological understanding. It is this: We must avoid any kind of biblicism which tries to make the testimony of scripture the only criterion for judging what is happening in the charismatic renewal. We believe that the scriptural witness is *one* primary norm for us; we also believe that the Holy Spirit has continued to instruct the Church down through the ages. To be unaware of, or to fail to take into consideration, what the Church has learned from her experience about the gifts of the Spirit is to see only part of the picture.

For example, we are going to see in this chapter that the Spirit was a felt reality in the lives of the first Christians; but we learn from the history of spirituality that people have become great lovers of God without such experiences. We are going to see many marvelous gifts of the Spirit at work among the early Christians; hopefully we will question ourselves as to why such gifts are not also present in our own lives (if they are not).

But it is possible to misunderstand the scriptures as to what these gifts are, how to acquire them, and how they function vis-a-vis the ecclesial community. Here history helps us. In Chapter 5, for example, we will see some aberrations concerning the gift of prophecy. What the Spirit taught the Church in the second century is meant for our instruction.

If scripture were our only guide, we might be tempted to be anti-intellectual in the wrong sense (Chapter 7). The Spirit at work in the history of the Church has blessed the use—and the rigorous use—of man's intellect as an aid in the understanding of revelation. The Catholic Church cannot be understood without Origen, Augustine, Aquinas, and Newman, just as it cannot be understood without Anthony of the desert, Benedict, Francis of Assisi, or the incredible Cure de Ars.

Jesus said that the Spirit would be with his Church always, not just during the first few decades of his Church. To simply wish to return to the bible alone as the exclusive norm for judging is to practically disregard this guidance of the Spirit throughout the ages. It is to disbelieve that the Holy Spirit has said anything significant during the two thousand years of Christianity. Keeping this in mind, let us turn now to the biblical witness.

It is said that old ideas are never really refuted; they simply give way to new experiences. While this may be an oversimplification, it is often true in our own lives. A new and powerful experience can, at one blow, reshuffle all our old mental patterns and notions.

This happened to the apostles and the early followers of Jesus. While they were with him they didn't understand too much. They weren't sure what he meant by the "kingdom of God," nor what his role in it would be. They couldn't fathom many of his parables, and they were scandalized by the mystery of the cross. But Jesus told them that when he left he would send them the Holy Spirit (Jn 14:26) who would clarify for them everything about himself and about his mission. And after the Spirit came, not only did they see him at work in their own lives but, reflecting back, they now saw the words and deeds of Jesus in a new light.

It is a commonplace now in our understanding of the New Testament to say that what we have in the gospels is a portrait of Jesus as seen through the faith-eyes of the early Christians. More, it is Jesus seen through eyes opened by the resurrection and the coming of the Spirit. The best way to review the New Testament witness to the action of the Holy Spirit is to see the interpenetration of all the principal documents—the gospels, Acts, and Pauline letters. They all flow from the new vision, from the new experience of the Spirit of Jesus.

This *experience of the Spirit* is the first fact which confronts us in the writings. The all-pervading, most striking feature about the first Christians, the most immediate impression one gets from even a superficial reading of the Acts of the Apostles and the letters of Paul, is that these people believed they were living under the direct guidance of the Holy Spirit.[1] They experienced a new consciousness, a new awareness, and a new power at work in them. And they attributed all these things to the Holy Spirit. The story of Pentecost (Acts 2) is Luke's account of his coming, and the writings of the New Testament describe how this powerful, creative, magnificent Gift of God was experienced in their lives. Before there was any clear doctrine of the Holy Spirit, there was the experience of the Spirit in the life of the community.

The Spirit was a "felt" reality: "Blind faith" with regard to the Spirit is a notion quite foreign to the New Testament. "And when they prayed, the place in which they were gathered *was shaken:* and they were all filled with the Holy Spirit" (4:31). "While Peter was still saying this, the Holy Spirit *fell* on all who heard the word" (10:44). "As I began to speak, the Holy Spirit *fell* on them just as on us at the beginning" (11:15). This tangibility, this concrete nature, as it were, of the Spirit's coming, finds its echo in the account of the Dove-Spirit descending on Jesus at his own baptism (Lk 3:22).

Now we begin our spiritual journey into the heart of the mystery of the Spirit's coming, presence and activity.

For the early Christians, an understanding of the Spirit's nature and role began in a new and startling way with their experience of the resurrected Christ. From that encounter their awareness of the Spirit grew and blossomed like a flower blooming into full beauty and radiance. It is precisely because Jesus has been raised by God that he becomes now a source of life for all who believe in him. "If you confess with your lips that Jesus is Lord and believe in your heart that God raised him from the dead, you will be saved" (Rm 10:9).

The explicit connection between the raising up of Jesus

and his power to hand over the Spirit is made in a variety of ways. Paul writes: "If the Spirit of him who raised Christ Jesus from the dead dwells in you, he who raised Christ Jesus from the dead will give life to your mortal bodies also through his Spirit which dwells in you" (Rm 8:11).

But more explicitly still it is John who is profoundly aware of the relationship between the resurrection-glorification of Jesus and the coming of the Spirit: "Whoever is thirsty let him come to me and drink. As the scripture says, 'Whoever believes in me, streams of living water will pour out from his heart.' Jesus said this about the Spirit, which those who believed in him were about to receive. At that time the Spirit had not yet been given, because Jesus had not been raised to glory" (Jn 7:37-39).

In the New Testament, Jesus is often described as the one who baptizes with the Holy Spirit. "For John baptized with water, but before many days you shall be baptized with the Holy Spirit" (Acts 1:5). "And John bore witness . . . he who sent me to baptize with water said to me, 'He on whom you see the Spirit descend and remain, this is he who baptizes with the Holy Spirit' " (Jn 1:33). "So John said to all of them, 'I baptize you with water, but one who is much greater than I is coming. . . .' He will baptize you with the Holy Spirit and with fire" (Lk 3:16).

In Luke's theology, among two of the most immediate effects of the Spirit's coming are the gift of tongues (Acts 2:4; 19:6) and boldness of speech in witnessing to Jesus as the Christ (Acts 1:8; 4:31).

Tongues is basically a gift of praise, a preconceptual speech whereby the person can freely express his aspirations to God. Paul lays down some guidelines for the use of this gift in community prayer services (1 Cor 14: 2ff).

Tongues, along with the gift of interpretation, is also one of the ways God can communicate his word to us (1 Cor 14: 26-33).

Along with opening their lips to praise God, the Spirit freed the early Christians from their fears of preaching boldly about Christ. "But the Spirit gave Stephen such wisdom that when he spoke they could not resist him" (Acts 6:10; cf. also 2:14).

Their new-found boldness threw light on some of the things Jesus had told them, and those who wrote the gospels reflect a consciousness of this new power. "And when they bring you to trial and deliver you up, do not be anxious beforehand what you are to say; but say whatever is given you in that hour, for it is not you who speak, but the Holy Spirit" (Mk 13:11; cf. also Lk 12:11-12; 21:14-15; Mt 10:17-20). "But when the Counselor comes, whom I shall send to you from the Father, even the Spirit of Truth, who proceeds from the Father, he will bear witness to me; and you also are witnesses, because you have been with me from the beginning" (Jn 15:26-27).

But the early Christians were not only aware of the Spirit's presence in times of danger and public witness. He was also their guide and helper in many *particular moments* of decision-making.

For example, in deciding who should be sent on a specific mission: "While they were worshiping the Lord and fasting, the Holy Spirit said, 'Set apart for me Barnabas and Saul for the work to which I have called them' " (Acts 13:2-3); in making decisions for the good of the community: "For it seemed good to the Holy Spirit and to us to lay upon you no greater burden than these necessary things . . . ." (Acts 15:28).

The Spirit is experienced as giving specific directions

at *important junctures* of the Christian apostolate: "And
the Spirit said to Philip, 'Go up and join this chariot'"
(Acts 8:29); "And while Peter was pondering the vision,
the Spirit said to him, 'Behold three men are looking for
you. Rise and go down, and accompany them without hesitation; for I have sent them'" (10:19-20); "And the Spirit
told me to go with them, making no distinction" (11:12);
"And they went through the region of Phrygia and Galatia,
having been forbidden by the Holy Spirit to speak the word
in Asia" (16:6).

If it is remembered that the Spirit also inspires visions
(Acts 11:5; 18:9; 7:55), and that his activity is also expressed by such phrases as "the angel of the Lord" (Acts
8:26; 10:3), we will understand better how the writers of
the gospels saw this same Spirit at work in preparing for
Jesus' coming, as well as operative at important turning
points in his life.

Thus, the Holy Spirit is very much at work in leading
Simeon to prophesy over the Child Jesus (Lk 2: 26ff). The
Spirit will make Mary fruitful (1:35). He warns of Herod's
desire to harm the Child (Mt 2:13) and thus is responsible
for saving his life. The Spirit beckons the Holy Family to
return from Egypt when the danger is past (2:19). And
when Jesus is about to begin his public ministry and con-
front head-on the powers of evil, it is the Spirit who leads
him into the desert to fast and pray (Mt 4:1).

Up to now we have referred mostly to Luke's theology
of the Spirit in the Acts of the Apostles. Historian as he
was, Luke saw the Spirit at work guiding the infant Church
outwardly as it made its way into the highways and byways
of the Mediterranean world.

It is in St. Paul, however, that we find the profound
mystical understanding of the Spirit's activity and role in

the *inner* life of the Christian. Paul also has a historical sense. He discusses the role of the Spirit in terms of past, present, and future. Briefly, his vision is this: "Having received what has been passed on, we cling to Christ in faith. As this becomes a matter of experience, we grow in what Paul calls 'knowledge' and 'wisdom,' and we experience the presence of the Spirit as the 'firstfruits' or 'pledge' or 'Promise' " (Martin). Paul's sense of time is more interior, more *moments of the soul's journey* than chronological time. It will serve as a useful outline for further discussion.

Our own resurrection, and therefore life in the Spirit, is frequently described by Paul in the *past* tense: ". . . *buried* with him in baptism, you *have been raised* up with him through faith in the power of God who raised him from the dead" (Col 2: 12-13). "If you *have been raised* up with Christ, seek the things that are above" (Col 3:1). "For by one Spirit we *were* all *baptized* into one body— Jews or Greeks, slave or free—and all *were made to drink* of the one Spirit" (1 Cor 12:13).

In speaking of our *present* resurrected life, Paul uses two phrases in connection with the Spirit—"in the Spirit" and "according to the Spirit." The former represents God's activity which places us in the mystery of Christ. By the latter phrase, Paul indicates that activity inspired in us by the Spirit to which we give our consent, and thus we act "according to the Spirit."

Thus he writes, "There is therefore now no condemnation for those who are in Christ Jesus . . . . But you are not in the flesh, you are *in the spirit* if the Spirit of God really dwells in you" (Rm 8: 1,9).

Another way to emphasize the same thing is to say that the Spirit *dwells in us:* "Do you not know that you are

God's temple and that God's Spirit dwells in you?" (1 Cor 3:16). The *you* in this quote is in the plural: Paul means that the whole community is the dwelling of the Spirit. But he writes the same to individuals: "Do you (singular) not know that your body is a temple of the Holy Spirit within you?" (1 Cor 6:19).

Paul's general way of describing the goal toward which the Spirit's action in us is tending is to say that the Spirit is working to conform us to the glorified Christ: "The Spirit himself bears witness along with our spirit that we are the children of God; and if children then heirs: heirs of God, coheirs with Christ, provided we suffer with him so that we may also be glorified with him" (Rm 8: 16-17). "He *will change* our weak mortal bodies and make them like his own glorious body . . . ." (Phil 3:21).

The "pangs of childbirth" is one of Paul's favorite images for expressing this longing for full maturity in Christ. The Spirit himself also seems to share in this "labor pain" with the rest of creation as everything pants toward freedom: ". . . all of creation groans with pain like the pain of childbirth. But not just creation alone; we who have the Spirit as the first of God's gifts, we also groan within ourselves as we wait for God to make us his sons and set our whole being free" (Rm 8:22-23).

The Spirit then who is already at work in us is the pledge of future fulfillment: "God has sealed us, and given us the pledge of the Spirit in our hearts" (2 Cor 1:22; cf. also 5:5; Eph 1:13-14).

Luke pointed out to us that tongues and boldness of speech were among some of the more observable manifestations of the Spirit's coming. Paul's insight is deeper, more inner-directed, certainly different. Paul looks into his *heart* and reflects on the Spirit's activity.

One of his first experiences is that the Spirit inspires him to *pray* in a new way, to relate to God with a more filial attitude: "God has sent the Spirit of his Son into our hearts crying Abba, Father" (Gal 4:6). The Spirit not only enriches his relationship to God, he helps Paul pray in his weakness: "In the same way the Spirit also comes to help us, weak that we are. For we do not know how we ought to pray; the Spirit himself pleads with God for us, in groans that words cannot express" (Rm 8:26). Paul exhorts his communities to cooperate with this prayer-action of the Spirit within them: "Pray in the Spirit with all prayer and supplication" (Eph 6:18).

It is very much part of the mind of Christ that the Spirit plays a distinct role in prayer to the Father: "Yet an hour is coming and is now here when the real worshipers will worship the Father in spirit and truth. And indeed it is just such worshipers that the Father seeks. God is spirit, and those who worship him must worship in spirit and truth" (Jn: 23-24).

Another element in Paul's new consciousness, flowing from the Spirit's action and presence, is wisdom—living knowledge of God's ways with man. "We speak a wisdom among the mature . . . . As it is written: 'What no eye has seen nor ear heard nor the heart of man conceived, what God has prepared for those who love him,' God has revealed to us through the Spirit. For the Spirit searches everything, even the depths of God . . . . Now we have not received the spirit of the world, but the Spirit which is from God so that we might know the things given to us by God" (1 Cor 2: 6-16, *passim*).

It is interesting to note that Paul writes later to some of the Corinthian "know-it-alls" that an awareness of the *partial* nature of the Spirit's activity is also a sign of the

Spirit! The Spirit inspires a kind of humility, a sense of not having the last word on everything. He gives intimations of depths still unfathomed.

Thus Paul experiences within him the Spirit crying "Abba" as well as a new wisdom of God's ways. What else does Paul experience? He experiences a new power to love. No, that is too mild. Paul experiences something much more profound. Somehow (it sounds presumptuous to say it) Paul experiences that he is able to love God and his brothers *with the same kind of love with which he himself is loved by God.* "The love of God is poured out in our hearts by the Holy Spirit who is given to us" (Rm 5:5). Paul's principle of morality is no longer any law external to him: There is a new law *in* him, a new source of action which leads to true freedom. The Holy Spirit himself is this new principle of life.

Love is not only for the individual. It is the lifeblood of the whole mystical Christ, the chief means whereby his body is built up: "If we live by the truth and in love, we shall grow in all ways into Christ, who is the head by whom the whole body is fitted and joined together, every joint adding its own strength, for each separate part to work according to its function. So the body grows until it has built itself up in love" (Eph 4:15-16).

The Spirit comes with many other gifts, charisms, to build up God's people into the body of the glorious Christ. They are the gifts being made more prominent today in the charismatic renewal. It may seem strange that, up until now, such extraordinary gifts as prophecy, healing, etc., have not even been mentioned.

This has been most deliberate. It is important to see these more "spectacular" charisms of the Spirit in relation to the resurrection, and always subordinate to and guided by the love each ought to have for the other. The whole point of Paul's magnificent hymn to love (1 Cor 13), one of the most beautiful passages in all of literature, is precisely to emphasize the fact that without love the other gifts are "nothing" (13:2) and "do (us) no good" (v. 3).

The same is the unmistakable teaching of the Lord, and we are well reminded of it before we come to a consideration of the other gifts. "But Lord, we prophesied in your name, cast out demons in your name, worked many miracles in your name. 'Amen I say to you, I do not know you. Depart from me, you workers of iniquity'" (Mt 7:22, 23). Jesus too is quite clear that love is the whole goal of all his teaching and striving (Jn 13:34).

The Spirit of Jesus is most lavish. He comes with many gifts to serve as aids in loving and in building up the body.

All gifts are for the body. Of course, the individual grows in love, but his personal growth and maturity are intimately bound up with others. "To each is given the manifestation of the Spirit *for the common good*" (1 Cor 12:7); "... he who prophesies speaks to men *for their upbuilding* and encouragement and consolation" (14:3); "He who speaks in a tongue edifies himself, but he who prophesies *edifies the Church*" (14:4); "When you come together, each one has a hymn, a lesson, a revelation, a tongue, or an interpretation. Let all things be done *for edification*" (14:26). "Edification" for Paul meant something much more than the modern connotation of the word. It meant to build up the body in love by serving one another. Gifts were for service, for the community, not for self-enjoyment or self-glorification.

In various places Paul lists what he considers to be these special gifts. We will see that some actions which we would tend to think are quite ordinary (for example, contributing money for the needs of others), Paul sees as a gift. His thinking is that only the Spirit of Jesus can infuse these actions with the proper dispositions. Hence they too are charisms, gifts.

"Having gifts that differ according to the grace given to us, let us use them: if *prophecy,* in proportion to our faith; if *serving,* in our serving; he who *teaches,* in his teaching; he who *exhorts,* in his exhortation; he who *contributes,* in liberality; he who *gives aid,* with zeal; he who does *acts of mercy,* with cheerfulness" (Rm 12:6-8).

"Now there are varieties of gifts, but the same Spirit; and there are varieties of working, but it is the same God who inspires them all in every one. To each is given the manifestation of the Spirit for the common good. To one is given through the Spirit the utterance of *wisdom,* and to another the utterance of *knowledge* according to the same Spirit, to another *faith* by the same Spirit, to another gifts of *healing* by the one Spirit, to another the working of *miracles,* to another *prophecy,* to another the ability to *distinguish between spirits,* to another various kinds of *tongues,* to another the *interpretation of tongues.* All these are inspired by one and the same Spirit, who apportions to each one individually as he wills" (1 Cor 12: 4-11). There are other gifts, but these are the principal ones.

It is not our purpose to comment on the nature and importance of all these gifts. Much literature is presently available on this subject. Perhaps the most significant thing we could say here is that all of them were very much part of the early Christians' experience of their new life in the Spirit, and there is nothing in the New Testament itself to indicate that these gifts were meant only for the first generations, to sort of "get things going."

The healing miracles of Jesus alone are too numerous to mention. That spiritual and bodily healing was part of the powers of the new age, and that the early Christians experienced this power is quite plain from the evidence of the New Testament.

Jesus said that his followers would do even greater signs than he (Jn 14:12). It was the faith understanding of Christians that the Spirit would confirm his presence by such signs: "Believers will be given these signs of power: they will drive out demons in my name; they will speak in strange tongues; if they pick up snakes or drink any poison, they will not be harmed; they will place their hands on the sick, who will get well" (Mk 16: 17-18).

Jesus himself points to such signs as a proof that the kingdom of God is now present in the world: ". . . it is God's spirit who gives me the power to drive out demons, which proves that the kingdom of God has already come upon you" (Mt 12:28). And it seems that *the* "sin against the Holy Spirit" is precisely to attribute to an evil spirit in Jesus what he is really accomplishing through the power of the Holy Spirit (Mt 12: 30-32). Evagrius of Pontus (4th-5th century) said beautifully that in some real way the kingdom *is* the Holy Spirit: "Your kingdom come: the kingdom of God *is* the Holy Spirit, and we pray to the Father so that he send the Spirit on us."

The first Christians understood that their experience of this magnificent Spirit through love, prayer, wisdom, miracles, prophecies, and gifts of all kinds was the sign that the last days prophesied by Ezechiel (36: 26-31) were at hand. Many understood this in a purely chronological sense, believing that the physical end of the world would happen soon. Future generations of Christians came to realize that, after Jesus, all days are last days. Time is no longer a straight line, a progression of historical events "leading somewhere." Jesus is now the center of all time; real time is to be headed deeper and deeper into the mystery of Christ who dwells within us, our "hope of glory" (Col 1:27).

Thus the experience of the Holy Spirit was very central in the life and thinking of Jesus and the early Christians. Tradition would wonderfully develop the theme. St. Irenaeus was fond of saying that Jesus and the Holy Spirit are the two arms of the Father by which he clasps us to himself. And, in a beautiful and succinct phrase, St. Athanasius sums up the very heart of the message: "The Word and Son of the Father, united with flesh, became flesh, the perfect man, so that men, united to the Spirit, might become one Spirit. So now he is God-bearing-flesh, and we are men-bearing-Spirit" (*On the Incarnation*).

Chapter 3

But He Will Baptize You With the Holy Spirit

— Mk 1:8

"Baptism in the Holy Spirit" is one of the catchwords of the charismatic movement. The phrase is new to the Catholic mind. This chapter presupposes some acquaintance with the literature on the subject, and attempts to shed some light on the nature and relationship of this phenomenon to Roman Catholic sacramental understanding and practice.

For the classical Pentecostals (those involved in this movement of the Spirit since the beginning of this century), baptism in the Holy Spirit is an experience of the Holy Spirit subsequent to a person's conversion to Christ and accompanied by the gift of tongues. In their view, this experience is not necessary for salvation, although God desires everyone to have its benefits. It is an experience to equip one for service in the Body of Christ.[1] The important points to remember about this approach for our purposes is that the baptism in the Holy Spirit is a definite experience, and that it is not necessary for salvation. A person can be *in Christ* without having had the baptism in the Holy Spirit as the classical Pentecostals understand it.

"Neo-pentecostals" is the name given to those in the other established churches who have taken on the spirituality of the charismatic movement as part of their faith approach. This is not to say that they have taken on the *theology* of the classical Pentecostals in all its aspects. Neo-classical Pentecostals have taken on its spirituality understood as a certain focus and emphasis. This focus "has to do with fullness of life in the Holy Spirit, the exercise of the gifts of the Spirit, directed toward the proclamation that Jesus is Lord, to the glory of the Father."[2]

For Roman Catholic neo-pentecostals, then, the baptism in the Holy Spirit is looked upon as a new empowering by the Spirit to witness, to grow in prayer and love of the scriptures, and to advance deeper into the Christian life. Generally this "baptism" is prayed for by a small group of people as they impose hands on someone. Our purpose is to try and situate this phenomenon in Roman Catholic thinking. A variety of theologies concerning the baptism in the Holy Spirit will continue to circulate in the movement as a whole, but each tradition should try and clarify it for its members in relationship to its own theological framework.

As a general stage-setting for our consideration of this phenomenon, try to imagine the sheer drama of the baptismal rite in the early centuries of the Church:

> Assembled in the halls of the great new basilicas, glittering with the newly kindled light of many lamps, they listened all night while the scriptures were recited from the reading desk or ambo. Toward daybreak the bishop and his ministers left the basilica for the baptistry, a spacious and splendid building, comprising not only the hall containing the font, but also dressing rooms for the candidates, and a separate chapel for the rites preceding baptism, and another

for the confirmation which followed it. The font itself was not an inconspicuous basin, but a large tank, often of fine marble, sunk into the floor of the building, into which the water might pour from jets along the sides. For the candidates were to stand in the water, and water was to pour over their bodies. In these circumstances and surroundings the candidates stripped; they renounced the devil; they were anointed for the final struggle with evil. They then descended into the font; they made the threefold act of faith and received the threefold pouring of the water, they were anointed with chrism, as being now kings and priests and in some sense Christs, since they shared his resurrection and his sonship. They then put on their white baptismal robes, and went before the bishop for the gift of the Spirit. The bishop prayed with hands outstretched over them; he implored the Father to send upon them the sevenfold Spirit of the Messiah, proclaimed by the prophet Isaiah. Having thus confirmed, or completed their baptism, he put the mark of Christ, the sign of the cross, upon their foreheads, and admitted them for the first time to the kiss of peace. In solemn procession the bishop and his ministers and the newly baptized returned to the waiting congregation in the basilica, and the Mass of the Christian Passover began in the full light of Easter Day.[3]

Turn your gaze now from this vivid drama to the realm of biblical theology. Consider the conclusions of a major scriptural work on the baptism in the Holy Spirit where the author summarizes the results of his study concerning the essentials of Christian initiation according to the New Testament:

. . . for the writers of the New Testament the baptism in or gift of the Spirit was part of the event (or process) of becoming a Christian, together with the effective proclamation of the gospel, belief in . . . Jesus as Lord, and water-baptism in the name of the Lord Jesus; that it was the chief element in conversion-initiation so that only those who had thus received the Spirit could be called Christians; that the reception of the Spirit was a very definite and often dramatic *experience,* the decisive and climactic experience in conversion-initiation, to which the Christian was usually recalled when reminded of the beginning of his Christian faith and experience.[4]

Do not these two things—the ceremony of the ancient Church, and this biblical theology—go neatly together? Is it not easy to see faith reaching a high point in the candidate's descent into and rising from the pool, and the Spirit crowning the whole holy night with a profound experience of his presence? Would it not be difficult for a person, properly prepared, to go through such an evening without experiencing a new birth?

Another of Dunn's conclusions is that each one of the essential factors in conversion-initiation (his phrase to describe the total event of becoming a Christian) has been overemphasized by one of the major "forces" in Christendom—Roman Catholic, Protestant and Pentecostal.

In Catholic doctrine, he says, the whole of initiation has come to be associated with the water-rite of baptism. The Protestants reacted to this emphasis and put the stress on personal faith. And now the Pentecostals, as a result of what they consider to be a new "in-breaking" of God on the world, put the emphasis on an *experience* of the Spirit.

Thus, Dunn says, in Christian initiation, the Catholic approach is disjoined from faith and the experience of the Spirit; in the Protestant approach faith is often severed from the water-rite and the experience; and now the pentecostal experience is separated from faith (in the sense that it is a nonessential moment *after* faith conversion) and often from water-baptism as well.[5]

Because of our interest in the baptism of the Holy Spirit in relation to Roman Catholic theology and practice, we confine our treatment to this aspect of the question. While the above conclusion by Dunn may be oversimplified, it is a useful distinction and insight to keep in mind as we approach this problem.

In the first place, it would not be possible to prove from New Testament texts the proper chronological sequence for these three elements—faith, water-baptism, the coming of the Spirit—in the process of becoming a Christian. The New Testament presents a variety of sequences:

> All claims to find this or that pattern for the performance of the sacraments in the New Testament fall to the ground. They were being administered before ever the New Testament was written. The method of their administration may be reflected in different passages in the New Testament; and there is no guarantee that they were administered everywhere in the same way. Passages in the New Testament may subsequently have influenced the method of their administration.[6]

Dunn himself, therefore, does not attempt any ideal chronological sequence. On the other hand, he does believe that some definite conclusions can be stated about the relationship and mutuality of these three realities:

> Faith demands baptism as its expression; baptism demands faith for its validity. The gift of the Spirit presupposes faith as its condition;

> faith is shown to be genuine only by the gift of the spirit.[7]

In short, he is saying that none of these elements can be separated from the others and still retain the comprehensive picture of Christian initiation as described in the New Testament documents.

As stated above, the ancient baptismal rite beautifully incorporated all these elements in the becoming of a Christian. As history proceeded, two changes, especially, began to break up this unity. One was the separation of the water-rite from the laying on of hands (separation of faith from the experience of the Spirit), and the baptism of infants (separation of faith and experience from the water-rite). The facts behind these developments are now well known, but a brief presentation of them here will not be out of place.

With the establishment of Christianity as the religion of the empire after Constantine, the becoming of a Christian and the making of a citizen were very much bound up together in the popular consciousness. In other words, to be a member of the Holy Roman Empire and *not* be baptized would be an anomaly. It is true that it was a very ancient practice for parents to bring their children to be baptized *along with them* when they were baptized. But as time rolled on, more and more Christian parents simply presented their children for baptism. "The Church finally consisted, with a few exceptions, only of those who had been baptized in infancy."[8] To be baptized as a baby, because of a variety of religious and cultural reasons, became the common practice.

The problem is that baptism, as depicted in the New Testament, is for adults; at least, that is the only context in which it is described and manifested to us. The connection now between the rite and a mature response of faith is blurred since babies cannot give a response. Neither do the words of the ritual change. They are still addressed as if to adults. Because of the solidarity of the family and the relationships between parents and children in the ancient and medieval world, the practice of saying that parents "answer for" their children becomes plausible.[9] It should be noted briefly here, and we shall return to this point, that such a historical development as here described does not necessarily mean a fortunate development as far as the Christian's *understanding* of his faith is concerned.

As regards the second separation, that of the water-rite from the bishop's imposition of hands, two factors especially played a major role. One was the growth in numbers of people, and the other was the geographical separation of many people from the place where the bishop was available.

In the East, this problem was given a better theological solution by leaving the ancient unity of the rite intact. The right to administer everything—baptism, anointing and confirmation—was simply given to the local presbyter. This same practice continued for a while even in the West in places such as Spain, Gaul, and even northern Italy. But in Rome, and in places more under its direct influence, the definite and traditional times for baptism (i.e., the Easter vigil) were retained, as well as the whole rite being performed by the bishop. Thus, for a while, it continued to be the practice to bring all children to the bishop for the total ceremony.

However, as time went on, Rome too had to face the problems of numbers and distances. The solution:

> The bishop's prayer with the laying on of hands was not restored to the baptismal rite, but became a separate rite of confirmation, and posed a problem for the medieval theologians to solve. The historical accident of separation has given the theologians a field day ever since.[10]

The coming of the bishop at a separate time from the baby's baptism became a distinct sacrament, that of confirmation. The present theological problem of relating the baptism in the Holy Spirit to the rite of initiation is part of the ongoing "field day" of theologians caused by this separation.

These historical facts are common knowledge today in sacramental theology. One of the disturbing aspects, however, of the above facts, is that the theology of the times seemed to have been used to *justify* the historical developments instead of *guiding* Church practice. If it is countered that such developments were not simply "historical" but were consciously allowed and fostered by theological viewpoints of the times (to which I would agree), then a similar approach could be justified again today, namely, that historical circumstances and prevalent theological viewpoints should again meet to make the present situation meaningful to Roman Catholic Christians. No age may be able to claim the perfect theology, but each age should have its own right to relevance. A theological approach in practice to baptism could be changed without denying the relevance and meaning of past approaches.

For example, in the case of infant baptism, history and theology met in the following way. Babies, as a matter of fact, were being baptized more frequently; some of the reasons have been mentioned above. But in the New Testament, baptism is concerned with the forgiveness of sins and a change of life, a conversion to Christ. Babies cannot sin. Of what, then, are they cleansed? Augustine develops and elaborates the teaching on original sin. It is the stain and effects of original sin that are washed away by baptism. Baptism is also the entrance by faith into the Christian community. Babies are not capable of this act of faith. So, this faith is "supplied" by the parents. The babies share in their parents' faith.

There is more involved here than what some might consider theological gymnastics coming to the aid of historical circumstances. The desire of parents to include their children within the protective ambit of grace in the Church's sacramental life is an important factor. Second-generation members of present-day communities, such as the Word of God community in Ann Arbor, Michigan, are baptized as infants. That is to say, young people who are involved in the charismatic renewal and who marry are led to have their children baptized, and it may not simply be the present practice of the Church which is the dominant and guiding principle. An instinct, an intuition, on the part of parents is deep within the fabric of mankind to surround their little ones with the Church's life.

However, having said this, it is the present author's conviction that such concern could be satisfied if the Church had some kind of acceptance rite, instead of baptism. It is getting more and more difficult for our theologians to explain just what happens at baptism of infants. Perhaps historical and cultural and theological factors are again converging which call for a different sacramental approach to baptism. If we could go from adult baptism to the baptism of babies, there is no reason why we could not go from the baptism of babies to the baptism of adults. It is not a matter of calling one more valid or more exact theologically than the other. It is a matter of allowing for and admitting a healthy pluralism in theology in the Church.

One example will suffice to show the kind of thinking we must indulge in to explain infant baptism today. It is taken from Father Kilian McDonnell's book quoted earlier.

He says there are two orders of reality. One is where God acts sovereignly by reducing his plan "to concrete history through the sending of the Son, the proclamation of the Good News, the establishment of sacramental ordinances such as baptism and the Eucharist . . . . There is another order of reality: man's historic and subjective appropriation of these redemptive acts."

> When the rite of initiation was experienced as an infant something really happened [first order]. But when this infant becomes an adult he must say yes or no to what was done to him as an infant. It is not possible for an adult to be a Christian by proxy. If the Catholic never says yes or no to his baptism then his relation to Christ is a form of cultural Catholicism; further it lacks a quality without which an adult cannot be a Christian, personal commitment [second order].[11]

It is becoming more and more difficult for this kind of theological reasoning to satisfy the modern inquirer. As long as the coming of the Spirit and the new birth are linked up with some kind of "first order" which is wholly unrelated to man's activity, everything else can only be seen as "further qualities" and not the very act by which man is born again.

To avoid any misunderstanding, it is not being suggested that *re-baptism* is advocated as the answer. That would be clearly heretical and divisive. Ideally, the present author would like to be included among the number of theologians mentioned by Kevin Ranaghan:

> There are a number of theologians today who argue that the Church should drop infant baptism and use adult or believer's baptism, not because infant baptism is invalid, but because they believe the needs of our day, the large number of baptized nonbelievers, etc., call for the establishment of a church of belief. But here again, it is a big difference between theological suggestion made within the Church, and vibrating through the Church (perhaps someday leading to a change in ecclesial practice), and the act of an individual discarding the doctrine and practice of the Church as it now stands (and as it has stood from the beginning of Christianity). There is a big difference between pushing for believers' baptism and practicing anabaptism (re-baptism). *The latter causes a break with the Church and, I believe, wounds the body of Christ.*[12]

There is no hope on the horizon that the Church will adopt, at least in the near future, the practice of adult baptism instead of infant baptism. Such a change, however, would neatly solve some of the present theological problems connected with the baptism in the Holy Spirit and situate this experience once again within the initiation of the adult Christian. Neither is it being suggested that practices should change so that theological problems can be solved! The problems are here already, caused by our own particular age's view of baptism, and by the finger of the Lord in the charismatic renewal, and many other factors.

Thus, in lieu of adult baptism, we are constrained to make such adult conversion and charismatic experiences "adjuncts" and "fulfillments" and "qualities" of sacraments received at an early age. "When the ordinary Catholic prays for 'Spirit-baptism' he is in effect praying for complete openness to the gifts and graces of his confirmation."[13] "The baptism of the Holy Spirit is a definite experience for more and more Catholics. They are experiencing the effects of confirmation. It is not that the Holy Spirit is being given to them for the first time. Rather, the power of the Holy Spirit is being released in their lives . . . ."[14]

One of the issues about which the Catholic theologian will have to come to a decision is whether or not an *experience* of the Spirit is part of God's plan for the total yes of the adult Christian. It is the opinion of the present author that such is the case. If one believes that the pentecostal movement is part of the Lord's providential plan for us, then it is precisely this experience of the Spirit which characterizes the whole movement.

Walter Hollenweger, who has published a nine-volume *Handbuch* on the movement, contends that the ultimate common denominator is "an overpowering sense of the presence of God and personal involvement, whether in the baptism by the Spirit or in worship around the Lord's table."[15]

We have already referred to Dunn's unambiguous conclusion: "Our examination of the New Testament evidence has shown that . . . the Spirit, and particularly the gift of the Spirit, was a *fact of experience* in the lives of the earliest Christians . . . ."[16] Other earlier works on the Holy Spirit, by authors renowned, all attest to the same inescapable fact. "No more certain statement can be made about the Christians of the first generation than this: they believed themselves to be living under the immediate government of the Spirit of God."[17] "The most immediate and striking impression regarding the origin and progress of early Christianity which we gain from the New Testament is the strong consciousness of the first believers of being under the power and direction of the Spirit of God."[18]

At the present time there is an unresolved ambiguity on the part of most Catholic authors to accept this fact of experience as part of Christian initiation.

Father Francis Sullivan says *both* of the following in the very same paragraph: "I am convinced that in the New Testament it was the normal thing for this initial outpouring of the Spirit to be a decisive experience . . . ." And further on: "On the other hand, a Catholic cannot doubt that in every valid and fruitful Christian initiation, the Holy Spirit is really given to the the new Christian, even though his coming is not experienced or manifested by perceptible signs."[19]

Simon Tugwell writes: "If a sacrament is an act of God in Christ, a *real* act, then it does its work even if we feel nothing—provided we are not blocking it. However, this is not to say that experience does not matter. If we read the New Testament, doesn't it rather suggest that all Christians are (not 'should be'; *are*) characterized by a kind of spiritual experience . . . they do seem to have known in their own experience the reality of the victory of Jesus Christ."[20]

Both writers must speak this way because they are trying to preserve the "objectivity" of the Catholic understanding of the sacraments, as well as accept the unquestionable evidence of the scriptures as regards an experience of the Spirit. We saw that theology came to the aid of historical development when babies became the common subjects for baptism. I'm sure that if conditions ever justified adult baptism in the Church, we would be able to find a new metaphysics and a new theology to speak more clearly about these matters.

Sullivan states the problem very neatly for us but answers it wrongly, I believe.

> [When] Catholic writers seem to accept from Pentecostals the view that only an *experienced* coming of the Spirit can rightly be called a "baptism in the Spirit" . . . they are putting the accent in the wrong place; they are taking as their criterion of "baptism in the Spirit" what is concomitant and secondary (the experience) rather than what is substantive and primary (the outpouring of the gift of the Spirit).[21]

Here, I believe, is the crux of the problem. The term "baptism in the Spirit" does not mean for anyone, either classical or neoclassical groups, the "substantive or primary" coming of the Spirit. As was mentioned in the beginning, even classical Pentecostals recognize the presence of the Spirit in a person who has not been "baptized in the Spirit."

Perhaps one of the most difficult subjects to analyze

by the human mind is how the Spirit can be received and abide in the new birth, and yet a further infilling can be realized in a subsequent experience. While the distinction may cause some perplexity for those who seek to understand this mystery through mental reasoning, no question remains with those who have entered and enjoy such experience.[22]

The baptism with the Holy Spirit is a definite experience.[23]

Sullivan confuses, in my mind, the "initial" gift of the Spirit (which he would say happens at baptism) with the baptism in the Spirit. It now seems quite evident from the historical, biblical and personal witnesses that we should definitely equate, unambiguously, baptism in the Spirit with the religious experience, and that this experience should be seen as *part* of God's plan for the *becoming* of a Christian. I believe that this is precisely what the Lord is saying to us in our time. I could not agree more with Dunn when he writes:

It is a sad commentary on the poverty of our own immediate experience of the Spirit that when we come across language in which the New Testament writers refer directly to the gift of the Spirit and to their experiences of it, either we automatically refer it to the sacraments and can only give it meaning when we do so, or else we discount the experience described as too substantive and mystical in favor of a faith which is essentially an affirmation of biblical propositions, or else we in effect psychologize the Spirit out of existence.[24]

Of all the elements of conversion-initiation described in the scriptures—water-baptism, conversion of life, faith, experience of the Spirit—we are having our greatest difficulty with the last. The time has come for Catholic theology to state quite plainly that an experience of God is part of his plan for our Christian initiation.

This is a bit of an aside, but it is important to remember that when we are speaking of such things as the coming of the Spirit or of our "initial reception" and so forth, we must remember that this is viewing the relationship from our perspective. In reality the Spirit does not "come and go" at all. When people are unbelievers, when we were still in the womb, before the water was poured, while it was poured, after it was poured, before we heard of Jesus, after we heard of Jesus, before we gave him our hearts, after we gave him our hearts, before an experience of the Spirit, after an experience of the Spirit, and on and on—the Spirit of the living God is always fantastically present and involved in our lives. It is *we* who go through changes in our relationship with him.

Tugwell relates a little story from the fourth century which fits in here very well. A monk was asked how he knew that he had been baptized. Perhaps his parents were pagan. He answered: "All who have received the divine Spirit in themselves (literally, in their womb) in holy baptism, are assured inwardly in their own heart that they have indeed been baptized, by the leaping and pricking of his grace, by the exultation and workings, by his, so to speak, jumping up and down in them. A woman does not just know by hearsay that she is pregnant!"[25]

It is not being implied that an experience is the foundation of faith. The foundation of faith is the *whole process* of true conversion, acceptance of Jesus, baptism into the community, and an experience of the Spirit's coming. According to the New Testament, no one of these should be in isolation of the other. When one of them is missing, the person's faith-foundation is deficient. To simply seek after an experience, for example, without any intention of changing one's life would be hypocritical, not to say dangerous.

Nor is it a matter of fostering a kind of Christianity which hankers after religious experience. In this connection writers often quote saints like John of the Cross and Teresa of Avila on the danger of seeking religious experiences. I don't believe these saints are talking about the fundamental experiences of the Spirit mentioned in the scriptures. They are warning mature Christians against seeking certain extraordinary manifestations such as visions and locutions. It seems biblically and theologically correct to say that God desires to give persons a fundamental experience of his presence as part of the whole process of Christian initiation-conversion.

It is becoming more evident, as the charismatic renewal progresses, that some people have had such a fundamental experience *prior* to their asking for the baptism in the Holy Spirit. This factor is important for our understanding of what the baptism in the Holy Spirit is theologically. Besides the personal testimonies related to me privately, I cite examples of two persons prominent in the charismatic renewal. They are Ralph Martin and David DuPlessis.

In a transcript of a discussion of the National Cursillo Secretariat concerning the relationship between the cursillo and the charismatic renewal, Ralph Martin was asked to explain, generally, what this charismatic renewal was all about. He said:

The claim is being made that what it is is a kind of renewal of baptism. Just a basic renewal of Christian baptism, commitment to Jesus Christ, and being filled with the Holy Spirit. *I think I experienced the pentecostal experience when I made my cursillo.*[26]

In a public talk at the National Convention at Notre Dame (1972), I heard David DuPlessis, often called the grandfather of the pentecostal movement, *look back* to an experience during a rainstorm when he was a boy in his teens as *his* pentecostal experience.

In short, these two men, prominent in the movement, do not necessarily regard the formal laying on of hands and the invoking of the Holy Spirit as their baptism in the Spirit. What they call their baptism in the Spirit is a fundamental, meaningful, conversion experience they had of God's presence. The experience being talked about here is not any kind of sweet feeling or extraordinary manifestation. It is a radical and fundamental experience which changes the whole direction and stance of one's life.

I would hold, therefore, that some Christians have had such an experience sometime during their lives as part of the process of their coming to know Christ. Some have built upon it and gone on to a deeper life in the Lord. Others, perhaps, did not recognize it for what it was, or did not give it any prominence in their lives—did not "claim it" as the Pentecostals would say. Most were never taught to expect such a visitation in any way, and so their Christian lives are lived without this experiential empowering which the Lord desires to give us to facilitate our life in the Spirit.

Sullivan, then, in my opinion, gives part of the answer to the problem when he writes: "In my opinion, it would be more correct to use the term 'baptism in the Spirit' only of that outpouring of the Holy Spirit which is the initiation of a *new* Christian into the life of the Spirit."[27] I would simply comment that the baptism in the Holy Spirit is not to be equated with the fundamental dwelling of the Spirit in the Christian, but is rather a radical experience of his presence which is meant to crown the whole process of a Christian's coming to live in Christ. Whenever and wherever this radical and fundamental experience of the Spirit's presence takes place, that is one's baptism in the Holy Spirit.

Some people are experiencing this tangible presence of the Spirit in the little ceremony of the laying on of hands. For others, this ceremony will be an occasion to rededicate themselves to Christ. For others, it will help to illumine their past and they will be helped to recognize more clearly just when the Lord did come to them and how they failed to recognize his presence and build upon it. Nor, as was said above, need we restrict the number of times the Lord can make us aware of his presence. The normal time for this experience would have been at the adult's Easter night initiation. Now, because of a variety of factors, the Lord must get in whenever and wherever he can!

Having said this, we do not wish to give the impression that there is not a new work of the Spirit being done in our times. It is not being implied that the charismatic renewal is simply pointing out what has always been happening in the lives of Christians. I believe that this is part of it. But the Spirit is also entering the lives of his people and releasing the gifts in a new and powerful way. It would be unfortunate if we simply adopted the "we've had it all before" attitude.

In the past we were never taught to expect and pray for

a crowning experience of the Spirit, nor were we taught to understand the gifts and pray for their release in us. This is a new lesson being taught us by the Spirit today. Therefore, it was possible to really have an inadequate initiation into the Christ life. To miss this point because of some triumphalistic attitude or superiority complex on the part of theologians and the Church would, it seems to me, miss the point of what the Spirit is saying to the churches in our times.

Finally, there is the question of whether Catholics ought to be using the term "baptism in the Holy Spirit." Tugwell describes the phrase as "unacceptable in the last analysis, being exegetically unsound, theologically confusing, and very risky pastorally."[28] There is much to what he says. The phrase "baptism in the Holy Spirit" appears nowhere in the New Testament. It is certainly not part of our Roman Catholic theological tradition. That it is confusing to people is an understatement. Even knowledgeable people involved for several years in the charismatic renewal do not know how to "fit it in" to their sacramental categories and traditional mind sets.

Kilian McDonnell is often quoted for his astute observation about "cultural baggage" and the charismatic renewal. Classical Pentecostals use styles of worship such as clapping of hands, raising of arms, etc., which are part of their cultural religious heritage. Other people—neo-pentecostals in the churches—need not adopt these mannerisms as part of the charismatic renewal. I believe that the phrase "baptism in the Spirit" is part of some "theological baggage" which was adopted simply because our Catholic theology had not yet caught up with what the Lord was doing. 'Tis ever so! I personally would like to see this phrase dropped, and to have the theological realities indicated by it worked into our whole catechetical approach to Christian initiation.

Be that as it may, books like this will not curtail the practice of using the term. Perhaps a much-neglected aspect of Christian initiation needs just such a label to make people sit up and take notice. But perhaps more and more we can put the emphasis not on the phrase but on the experience of God's presence, wherever and whenever that has happened to us. This, I think, is the essential point and should not be watered down. The Lord does not need labels to work among us; but if keeping the label helps to emphasize, for a while, this aspect of his ways with us, then retaining it will cause no great harm. The danger to be aware of is confining this experience of the Spirit to a certain ceremony.

To sum up. The ideal would seem to be that the moments of coming to Christ—conversion, faith, water-baptism, experience of the Spirit—should take place sacramentally in the life of an adult Christian. In lieu of this, we must continue to explain moments of mature faith and experiences of the Spirit as "fulfillments" of sacramental moments. This is not such an unreal approach. After all, we are dealing with life-processes. When does a flower become a flower? When does it pass from one stage to another? When does a baby become a boy and a boy a man?

Theologically, the phrase "baptism in the Holy Spirit" should refer to the first time the person who has accepted Christ experiences, in a radical and fundamental way, the presence of the Lord in his life through the power of the Holy Spirit. This experience should be seen as biblically sound, as something valid, something to be hoped for and prayed for. In God's plan it seems that he wants to give us this fundamental experience to start us off on our journey toward him in Christ. The mature Christian does not seek after religious experiences. The Lord desires to lead us on to things much more mature than simply relishing his presence.

There are valid objections to the continued use of the phrase "baptism in the Holy Spirit" from a Roman Catholic point of view. It may well be part of the theological baggage that Catholics have simply taken over from Pentecostalism. It perhaps was and still is justified to use such a phrase since Catholic theology did not and has not yet integrated the reality behind this phrase into its thinking on Christian initiation. But instead of emphasizing the label we should unequivocally incorporate the reality of the experience into our catechetical programs, i.e., the reality of God's desire to give us a real experience of his presence as part of our total initiation into the Christ life.

Chapter 4

Test Them to Find Out if the Spirit They Have Comes from God

— 1 Jn 4:1

Charismatic renewals are not new to the Church, though whether the present one is greater in both magnitude and quality only time will tell. It is a trite though nonetheless true statement that an ignorance of history leads to a repetition of its mistakes. We have much to learn from Church history. It is hoped that the present chapter will show the value of such knowledge, and perhaps encourage the reader to investigate aspects of Church history which deal with the charismatic.

Frequently in books and articles concerning the charismatic renewal reference is made to Montanism, a charismatic explosion in the second century. The movement derives its name from a man named Montanus who lived in a village called Ardaban in that part of Mysia adjoining Phrygia. Phrygia was the recognized center of ecstatic religion in the pagan world. Possibly Montanus was a converted priest of Cybele, and most authors date his strange prophesying about the year 172-173.

Montanus believed in a new and revolutionary descent of the Holy Spirit who would now perfect what had only been begun in the apostolic period. Tertullian, an early and distinguished Christian writer who later became a

Montanist, even made the distinction between the coming of the Spirit at Pentecost and the coming of the "Paraclete" in Montanus.

To show that some kind of uniqueness was claimed, Tertullian distinguished four stages in God's revelation to us: natural religion, the Old Testament, the gospel of Christ, and the revelation of the Paraclete in Montanus. "The essential principle of Montanus," states the *Encyclopaedia Britannica*, "was that the Paraclete, the Spirit of Truth whom Jesus had promised in the gospel of St. John, was manifesting himself to the world through Montanus and the prophets and prophetesses associated with him." The emphasis was on a completely new age, in some way perfecting and even superseding the apostolic age.

In the area of prophecy, Montanus' claim was not simply to a renewal of this charismatic gift in the Church. (It is provable from the documents of the times that prophecy was still extant in the Church of the second century.) Montanus' claim was to a *new source* of revelation, hitherto unknown in the Church.

In the area of church discipline there were conflicts over the right to absolve from sin and the exercising of clerical functions by the laity. On a more superficial level, the Montanists were accused of being anti-intellectual, and of making oversevere demands in their moral discipline. They were labeled as "divisive" in the community of believers. Finally, they gave the impression of being "super-Christians" to distinguish themselves from the merely "natural" Christians.

Briefly, then, what the Church of the second century rejected was: 1) any hint of a new revelation that could supersede the scriptures (from the debates of the times it is clear that the Montanists equated the writings of its prophets as being on a par with the scriptures); 2) the teaching that Montanus and his followers were the *last* of all the prophets (Maximilla, one of the prophetesses, stated: "After me there will be no prophecy"); 3) that the Spirit had now come in a new age of revelation, somehow superior even to the apostolic age; 4) the ecstatic nature of prophesying.

Eusebius, an early church historian, wrote, in reference to the Montanists: "The false prophet speaks in a trance, which induces irresponsibility and freedom from restraint; he begins by deliberate suppression of conscious thought and ends in a delirium over which he has no control." Though Eusebius was a stalwart churchman and often exaggerated his remarks, it is probably true that the prophesying of the Montanists was of such a nature. Utilizing some of my own experience in the charismatic renewal and examining some of the literature available today, some attempt will be made to offer tentative answers to the question as to whether the charismatic renewal is a new Montanism.

In talking and listening to people involved in the charismatic renewal one certainly hears about this new and wonderful thing that the Lord is doing among his people. When a person's life in Christ comes alive, it is difficult for him not to think and speak about it as a *new* reality in his life. That is quite a different thing, however, from transposing this personal experience onto the universal life of the Church in our age and speaking of a "new age" of the Church. The phrase could even be acceptable if one meant a new burst of life in the Church, as long as it does not mean what the Montanists meant, a completely new stage of revelation.

In the writings of Catholics, where some theological

distinctions are made, there is nothing approaching this "completely new age" of the Montanists. The evaluation of Father Edward O'Connor, professor of theology at the University of Notre Dame, is typical of a Catholic's understanding of this *new* outpouring:

> Belief in the Spirit means belief that Jesus Christ is not merely a dead hero, nor a great seer whose doctrine still enlightens and inspires mankind, but a Lord who actually and effectively rules his people. There is nothing new in this belief; it is part of the primitive and fundamental teaching of the Christian faith. But this is precisely the point: the Pentecostal movement is *not characterized by a new doctrine on the Holy Spirit* (emphasis added), but by the fact that traditional doctrines have come to life with a new freshness and vigor.[1]

"New" can have various meanings. Something can be new for me without being new for the Church. Something can be new in the sense of an old reality having been forgotten or neglected and now remembered or returned. Or, new can be the completely new, the "never having happened before." The charismatic renewal is generally understood in the first and second senses, and not as a completely new stage of revelation or of the Spirit's activity.

Much of the commotion connected with Montanism revolved around the issue of prophecy. The prophesying of the Montanists became a kind of direct and detailed guidance of the Church by the Spirit. Probably the main reason for Tertullian's going over to Montanism was that this kind of prophecy gave the Holy Spirit a continuing teaching function in the Church. The Montanists believed that points of both discipline and doctrine might receive correction through the continued action of the Spirit in the Church.

Put in this way, such a role for the Spirit doesn't sound so bad. Isn't it true that the Spirit continues to guide the Church? Yes. But a further penetration into the nature of the gift of prophecy will show how the Montanists misunderstood this gift and abused it to try and force the Church into a new kind of bondage.

Those involved in the charismatic renewal believe that the Spirit is pouring out his gifts on his people. Prophecy is one of these gifts. The following characteristics of prophecy are taken from a series of articles by Derek Prince, an internationally known teacher in the charismatic renewal. He is not a Roman Catholic, but his thinking on the theology of the gift of prophecy is representative of the best insights current in other churches. Many Catholics, prior to popular theological reflections by their own theologians, have appropriated this teaching of classical Pentecostals such as Prince. We quote only those characteristics most pertinent to our present subject:

1. The end purpose of all true prophecy is to build up, to admonish, and to encourage the people of God;
2. All true prophecy always agrees with the letter and and spirit of scripture;
3. All true prophecy centers in Jesus Christ, and exalts and glorifies him;
4. True prophecy, given by the Holy Spirit, produces liberty, not bondage.[2]

Several points should be mentioned here concerning the difference between these features of prophecy and the nature of prophecy among the Montanists.

Unlike the Montanists, any hint today, whether inside or outside the Catholic Church, that a prophecy could be put on the same level with the scriptures would be unthinkable. Secondly, prophecy exalts Christ and not other people, charismatic leaders or otherwise. Montanus seems to have become the center of another cult. Some of his prophecies handed down to us are: "I am the Lord God omnipotent dwelling in man." "I am neither an angel nor an envoy, but I the Lord God, the Father, have come." "I am the Father and the Son and the Paraclete." Such statements were a bizarre form of Christian prophecy, to say the least.

Third, and most importantly, true prophecy produces liberty. In explaining this, Prince comments: "The gift of prophecy is an extremely powerful spiritual instrument either for good or for evil. Through exercise of this gift, an unscrupulous person can bring others into bondage to himself and can thus establish what is virtually a spiritual 'dictatorship.' It is vitally important to understand that in the body of Jesus Christ, there are no 'dictators.' "[3] The words of prophecy are not words of bondage, legalistically binding someone to a definite manner of action. This is an extremely important point.

In the author's opinion, one tendency of the pentecostal movement which could be labeled as "dangerous" would be this misuse of the gift of prophecy in giving detailed directives to people, and also in predicting the future for them in the name of the Lord. A few words of explanation about this.

One of the general theological dangers in the pentecostal movement is a completely fundamentalist approach to the scriptures. A fundamentalist approach, in the bad sense, is a refusal to take into consideration any exegetical tools in attempting to understand what the scriptures mean; it consequently is reduced to an overliteral interpretation which frequently results in contradictions. A nonfundamentalist approach is often equated with a lack of faith in God's word, and with a watering down of revelation. That can happen, and frequently does. The pitfall of the fundamentalist is that he often believes in the wrong things; the pitfall of the nonfundamentalist is often that he believes in too few.

Scripture, then, is to be considered neither an extraordinarily difficult book to understand nor an easy book. It can be more fully understood if one will take the ordinary means required to understand any book written over 2,000 years ago. Few will deny that a book written that long ago requires a little study.

With regard to prophecy, for example, it is possible for some people who come into the pentecostal experience to equate prophecy with predicting the future. This interpretation can be had from several places in the scriptures, e.g., Old Testament prophets, certain passages in the gospels, some passages in Acts. It is not the place to exegete such passages here. But it is common knowledge in scripture studies today that *prophecy has little to do with predicting the future.* A scholar, such as the late Abraham Heschel in his masterful work on *The Prophets,* has next to nothing to say about prophecy as predicting the future. In his summary, he talks about the prophets' divine attentiveness and concern and of the prophets' identification with God's view of the world.

In the Pauline epistles, from which sources persons involved in the charismatic renewal draw most of their guidelines for the gifts, prophecy is mostly *exhortation.*[4]

More sources could be quoted. The point is that explicit prediction of the future under the Spirit's guidance is on very shaky ground in modern scripture studies. Persons less familiar with the meaning of scripture may simply mimic what they think is God's ways with us by attempting to predict the future because they think this is what prophecy is. Prophecy *is* a gift of the Spirit, but it is not to be equated with giving people detailed instructions about the future.

I give one example of what I mean from personal experience. In talking with a young person who had been involved with a group of Jesus people, she described how their leader led the group for almost a year with detailed predictions of where they were to go, what city they were to stay in, and so on. This is no moral judgment of the leader, but such behavior exhibits a gross misunderstanding of the Spirit's relationship to us according to the New Testament. For St. Paul, prophecy was inspired speech which built up—edified—the community, and this mostly by convicting the hearts of the hearers. It had little or nothing to do with a detailed program for future actions.

A healthy trend in the writings of the charismatic renewal concerning prophecy is the insistence that its contents be judged by the community. This prevents the kind of "dictatorship" mentioned by Derek Prince. Father Donald Gelpi, S.J., writes: "Although the gift of prophecy must be held in high esteem by all Christians, the value of any given prophecy . . . must be tested reflectively by the community in union with its official leaders."[5] This refers to both the intimate prayer group to which one belongs (concerning specific matters) and also to the wider community of the Church (as regards matters of doctrine). The Montanists would not subject their prophecies to the judgment of the Church at large and its official leaders.

Any emphasis on the gifts of the Spirit in the Christian community naturally leads to an emphasis on the ministry of all believers since the gifts are precisely for the community. In Montanism, mostly in reaction to the growing solidification of ministerial functions, its members began to exercise many functions of the clergy. (It is fairly certain historically that they allowed women to baptize and to celebrate the Eucharist.) At a time when the Church was becoming more and more of a fixed ecclesiastical structure, it was inevitable that such a trend among the Montanists would find strong opposition. Is there a trend in the charismatic renewal today for laity to assume the functions of the clergy?

It is true that in the charismatic renewal, because of the gifts, there definitely are ministries of healing, prophecy and teaching among the laity. Gifts were meant to be used and are being used. It is a matter of one's theology whether he describes such activity as "supplementing" or "supplanting" the work of the clergy. Father O'Connor uses the word "paraclericalism" to refer to lay leadership developing in such ways as to "duplicate or supplant the functions proper to the ordained ministry."

Even in the normal state of the Church, the exercise of gifts such as teaching, prophecy and healing cannot be labeled as clerical functions, although in a general sense it is true to say that such ministry requires at least tacit approval. The recent trend on the Church's part to return the minor orders to the laity is, it seems to me, a recognition of gifts among the laity which need to be given official approbation by the Church. However, the general understanding of clerical or priestly functions refers to the celebration of the sacraments, properly so called. To the best of the author's knowledge, neither in theory nor in practice do those involved in the charismatic renewal engage, in any appreciable degree, in this formal celebration of the sacraments without an ordained priest.

The greatest danger at the present time is not this paraclericalism. As the official statement of the American bishops noted, Catholics involved in the charismatic renewal welcome and desire the involvement of the clergy to assist in understanding and coordinating these gifts for the good of the whole Church. It seems that the greatest danger at the present time in this area stems from the clergy—the neglect of the clergy to help these people work out the relationship between their gifts and the official ministry of the Church. Without this clerical involvement and concern, paraclericalism could become more serious.

Explosions of the Spirit are often infected by several unhealthy tendencies. Montanism had them, and the present charismatic renewal has them. Whether such tendencies will grow out of proportion and prove harmful to the movement and to the Church, only time will tell.

One of these tendencies is the wrong kind of anti-intellectualism. Origen accused the Montanists of "intellectual weakness," and Hippolytus called them "uncritical." Granted, these are not the worst evils in the world, but they betray tendencies which, if not checked, could cause harm in the long run.

It is often heard in the charismatic renewal, either implicitly or explicitly, that "reason cannot save"—and this, not so much from prominent leaders as from the "rank and file." It is certainly true that reason cannot save. But too often people will quote from Romans and equate St. Paul's "wisdom of this world" with the power of the intellect and see some kind of positive good in not thinking. "One may not simply equate the wisdom of the world (or of this age) with reason. . . . The 'wisdom of the world' is a very definite way of thinking, qualified by its content. (Further on) in fact, he (Paul) makes very powerful use of reasoned arguments in his letters. . . ."[6]

It should not be forgotten that reason too is a gift from the Lord, one of the greatest we have. Its neglect in areas where it should be brought to bear cannot be encouraged. If the charismatic movement is from the Lord (as I believe it is), then reason and study under the guidance of the Spirit will only help to make his work shine out more clearly.

In a section of his book entitled "Principles Concerning the Pentecostal Movement," Father Gelpi rightly reminds Catholics of the validity of bringing the intellect to bear on what is happening:

> No finite human attempt to theologize the Pentecostal experience is closed to critical reflection.

> Theologizing the Pentecostal experience enriches it, provided that theological reflection preserves a sense of its initial grounding in the Pentecostal experience and a sense of its responsibility for providing intellectual direction for the activity which flows from that experience.

> Theologizing the Pentecostal experience enhances it by focusing the mind's attention on limited aspects of that experience, but it does so at the risk of oversimplifying the experience itself.[7]

"Theologize," in the above-quoted statements, simply means the use of our intellect in trying to understand the activity of the Lord in our lives. The last statement in particular reminds us of the dangers of the intellect, its capacity to rob experience, in this case religious experience, of its richness. We unconsciously tend to equate our thoughts with reality, a phenomenon known as "reification" in philosophy. Pointing out the dangers of the intellect simply reminds us that all the gifts have destructive and constructive capacities. Balance and their proper use—not neglect—is the key.

Hans Kung says that Montanism was of a separatist and sectarian nature. It really had in mind the formation of a new community of Christians, detached from "lax" Christians.[8]

It is understandable and even necessary that people with similar faith needs come together for mutual support. No one should label as "sectarian" the fact that people involved in the charismatic renewal have their own prayer meetings and even their own national conventions! Such meetings are usually open to anyone who wishes to come. Again, to quote Father Gelpi: "Every authentic charism seeks to build up and strengthen the community. Hence, no charismatic movement which is deliberately factionalistic in its intent comes from the Spirit of Christ."[9]

Tendencies to meet together of people in the same movement are quite normal; in fact, such meetings are one of the components of any movement. What should be avoided in the charismatic renewal is *overmuch* banding together for liturgies, apostolic works, and so on. The tendency always should be to enter into and enrich the existing activities of the Church and to bring them new life. Ralph Martin, one of the national leaders in the movement, has precisely this integration as one of his constant themes. He sees one of the goals of the movement as an acceptance

on the part of the wider Church community of these gifts
of the Spirit, so they can help to revivify all the dimensions of Church life. This seems also to be a concern of
many involved.

In connection with the sectarian spirit the Montanists
made distinctions between "psychical" and "spiritual"
Christians. Montanists, needless to say, were of the latter.
Any such categorization, any kind of "us" and "them"
mentality is particularly repugnant in the followers of Jesus.
St. Paul makes it very clear that possession of the gifts is
not necessarily a sign of holiness. It is possible to be working miracles in the Lord's name and still be unknown to the
Lord. Only the Lord knows who is living by his Spirit.
Thus even the phrase "have you received" (in reference to
the baptism in the Holy Spirit) is repugnant to Catholic
ears and does not reflect the subtleties of our understanding
of God's work in us.

As a movement which claimed to restore the power of
the Spirit, Montanism fell into a new legalism. Sexual
purity and the renunciation of the pleasures of life were the
demands of the new prophets. Sexual purity and a healthy
asceticism are fine, but the Montanists went one better and
forbade second marriages (after the death of the first
spouse) and absolution could not be given to adulterers
and fornicators. Also, more fasts were imposed as binding on all.

A heightened sense of the Spirit in our lives is often
accompanied by a more pronounced need for discipline and
penance. Those involved in the charismatic renewal (but
not these only) also experience the need for greater self-
denial, e.g., fasting. There is nothing wrong with such
tendencies; they have always been part of the Christian life.
(One might wish, though, to have a good discussion on

what constitutes real rigorism in the life of the Spirit.) The mistake of the Montanists (and often of enthusiasts in general) was to try and impose their notion of rigorism on the rest of the Church.

Part of the genius of the Church is that it allows many levels of ascetical expression to coexist, and does not impose identical standards on everyone. When "my" inspiration starts to become a standard for everyone else, a new type of bondage is being substituted for the old. The Lord calls each of us by name, and we are responsible for answering our individual call. "When Peter saw him [John] he said to Jesus, 'Lord, what about this man?' Jesus answered him, '. . . what is that to you? Follow me!' " (Jn 21:21-22).

It would be true to say that many of the unhealthy tendencies which existed in Montanism in the second century exist today in the charismatic renewal in varying degrees. Whether any of them will assume unnatural proportions and lead to deeper aberrations—sects and heresies as yet unnamed—only time will tell. The question posed before—Is the charismatic renewal a new Montanism?—at least for now, can be answered with a definite "No." The Church certainly has been through enough enthusiastic movements to be able to discern the Spirit of Jesus. Hopefully, too, all those involved in the charismatic renewal will learn from history, from movements like Montanism, how to enrich and revitalize the Church without rending her asunder.

Before we conclude this chapter, it may be of interest to the reader to get a view of the overall effect of Montanism on the subsequent history of the Church. Montanism was not strictly speaking a heresy. It erred more in proportion than in substance. Some authors even think that the Church remained pretty much what it was, despite Montanism. However, this does not seem to be the case. The dictum, *Abusus non tollit usum* (abuse does not take away use) is, as Msgr. Ronald Knox reminds us, good law but bad history. Reactions to abuses in life often cause serious overreactions.

The Church seems to have suffered loss in two areas, in that of congregational prophecy and in the spiritual independence of the laity.

The gift of prophecy was driven into a corner and became suspect. "In vain did Irenaeus warn his contemporaries against driving the true prophecy out of the Church from anxiety over the false. In opposition to the boastful parading of revelations the tendency is to rely more and more on rational and didactic forms of spiritual utterance. The era of prophets draws to a close . . . indeed the very word falls slowly out of use."[10] Irenaeus was Bishop of Lyons about 180 A.D. He is still able to express himself quite positively in regard to prophecy and the gifts of the Spirit.

On the other hand, Origen (185-254 A.D.), the Church's first real systematic theologian, already *looks back* to a period after which the Spirit's gifts in the Church ceased. Also at this time, the phrases "the Law and the Prophets *up to John*" and "the complete number of the prophets" begin to appear in documents.

The conflict between Montanism and the Church was not so much a conflict between a charismatic Church and a hierarchic Church (which need not be opposed to each other), as between two concepts of the Church—a Church of "regular channels" and a Church of "gifts through spiritual persons." After Montanism there was a distrust of free spirituals who were not sanctioned by authority. With the deemphasizing of charisms, the Spirit was seen to guide the Church through the newly formed canon of scripture and through ecclesiastical offices properly established. And, because of the usurpation of priestly functions by the Montanists, there was an even tighter control on ecclesiastical functions.

Whether these overreactions were the work of the Spirit is another question, but if it is permissible to make a judgment of a particular movement in history that it was "not of the Spirit," then Montanism seems to have been such a movement. Its chief teachings—the final age of prophecy, final age of the Spirit, the imminent second coming (the exact time and place were predicted, and whole communities left everything and wandered around the region in frenzied expectation)—these were simply not the needs of the Church in the second century. As subsequent history proved, neither were they part of the Lord's plan.

Moreover, Montanism's human origins become obvious when we consider the content of its prophecies and the way the gift of prophecy was abused, not to mention the harm caused to the Church as a whole. If Montanism began in the name of the Spirit, it certainly ended by tightening the "screw of legalism."

We should not be too hard on these early enthusiasts in the Church. In the great diversification of early Christianity, and considering the obstacles of geography, unclarified doctrines, and many other factors, they seem to have been motivated by a real concern for the freedom of the sons of God. While they might have lacked wisdom, they did not lack enthusiasm. And while enthusiasm may not be the only virtue, neither is it the greatest vice.

Chapter 5

In the First Place Apostles, in the Second Place Prophets

— *1 Cor 12:28*

The notion of prophetic and charismatic elements having a prominent and respectable place in the life of any Christian community is a relatively new idea for many priests and religious. It is not a new idea *for the Church,* but for the communities within the Church in the period before the Second Vatican Council. The guiding principles during this latter period were the directives coming "from the top down" and there was no question that this was the divinely appointed way of ordering the Christian community.

Cardinal Suenens posed for himself the question as to what really was the core idea, the "seed of life," as it were, around which the pastoral directives of the Council were centered:

> If we were to be asked what we consider to be that seed of life deriving from the Council which is most fruitful in pastoral consequences, we would answer without any hesitation: it is the rediscovery of the people of God as a whole, as a single reality; and then by way of consequence, the coresponsibility thus implied for every member of the Church.[1]

One of the heartbeats of Vatican II's message to the Catholic world is that each and every member of the Church assumes in practice his or her rightful place as a member of the Body of Christ, living by his Spirit, and that each of us use his gifts for the building up of the body. It is a cry to end all passivity, and a directive to those in authority to remind them that one of their primary functions is to discern and encourage the gifts of all those in the community, so that all gifts may be used for the total good of all.

We believe that this theological position of the Council was made under the guidance of the Spirit, as were all the statements of the Council. It is the present author's opinion that now, in the charismatic renewal and in many other movements in the Church, the Spirit is equipping his people with gifts of many kinds, so that the theological statements of the Council might become actual reality.

We shall see in a subsequent chapter (7) some of the problems connected with the charismatic renewal entering a community structure. We saw briefly how Montanism, a charismatic explosion in the second century, was partly responsible for the gradual decline of the prophetic and charismatic dimensions in the Church. The present chapter, utilizing some of the findings of a significant patristic study,[2] attempts to offer some insights into the relationship between office and charisma in the first centuries of the Christian era.

Throughout his study, the author is concerned with tracing the development of the relationship between the phenomena of office and charism (or free spiritual authority). The present chapter is, therefore, not very creative, but an attempt to share with the reader certain themes which seem to us especially important and suggestive for the growth of Christian community in these "charismatic times."

One of the perennial temptations of enthusiastic

Christians, and it has cropped up in every age of the Church's life, is the attempt to return to the pristine and original fervor and format of the early Christian community. The desire to live the Christian life as simply and as generously as the first Christians is a most laudable and wonderful inspiration. It is truly a mark of the Spirit. The only problem is, *"What* first Christians?"

From Von Campenhausen's study, and other similar studies,[3] one fact is becoming abundantly clear: There was a great deal of variety in early Christianity, both in doctrine and in practice, and variety also in the forms and configurations of Christian communities.

If one is in search, for example, of the *ideal Christian community,* it is quite evident from his study that *such a phenomenon never existed.* This is not to say that there were no Christian communities where real love and concern prevailed, and where all lived deep lives together in Christ. No. What is being denied is that *there was only one definite way of structuring such a community.* The author contends that it would be hazardous to take our model for community from any *one* of the biblical writings in isolation of the other testimonies. At the very end of his study he writes: "In looking for a rationale of authority, therefore, we come round to the fact that the answer and the direction are not to be found in the inadequate fragments, but must be elaborated on the basis of the biblical testimony as a whole."[4]

Those who are impelled by the really beautiful longing to return to the form and style of the first Christian community often make the mistake of selecting only certain elements from a total picture. Usually they zero in on Paul's more charismatic communities as described in 1 and 2 Corinthians. Our author's conclusion, which it is good for us to appreciate from the very outset, is that not only were there a variety of structures (ranging from Paul's more charismatic communities to the Judaeo-Christian types modeled more on the system of elders), but that in order to get a picture of the elements necessary for true Christian community, one must pay attention to *all* the writings concerning the communities of the first centuries.

We cannot only read the Letters to the Corinthians and disregard the pastoral epistles (Timothy, Titus, etc.), or vice versa. The charismatically inclined must pray over and study the structures evidenced in Timothy, and the office and hierarchically inclined must pray over and ponder the nature of the Corinthian communities. Aberrations are due to this failure to pay attention to either office or charisma.

The basic lesson for us in the present study is to avoid searching for *the* model of the relationship of charisma and office. The best we might be able to do is attempt to understand some of the principles of Christian community in this area, which we can then adapt to our own situations. The danger ever with us is to concentrate on any one model in scripture to the exclusion of others. In this way, one ends up by "giving exclusive rights either to the Spirit as opposed to office, or to office instead of Spirit."[5]

We have been using the word "office" and "charisma" in a very general sense, and they will remain thus. "Office" will refer to the more permanent and stable elements of community formation such as tradition, officeholders, bishop, in short, the images which naturally occur to us when the word "office" is used. "Charisma" will refer to the more elusive elements such as Spirit, charisms, prophetic voice, free men of the spirit, etc. It is really the philosophical problem of the ages, the relationship between

permanence and change. We know that both are necessary, but how are they to be conceived and lived out in
practice?

We turn our attention first to the little community
around the Lord. It is a unique group. The structure of
their community is completely determined by the person of
Christ. Jesus claims no "official backing" for his words
and his teaching *except his own person*. He can say and
do what he says and does because he is who he is. His
authority is vindicated by his action, that is, it is demon-
strated. Jesus unites in his person both office and charisma,
both authority and the demonstration of spiritual power.
He needs no further justification for his actions than himself, and he displays spiritual power to confirm what he says
and does.

When he is questioned as to his right to forgive sins,
he heals (Mk 2:7-12); and when asked if he thinks he is
greater than Jacob, he simply reveals the secrets of hearts
(Jn 4:12-30). The Jewish elders continually want to know
"by what right" Jesus does all these things (Mt 21:32).
Jesus never gives them a direct verbal answer, but demon-
strates his right by what he does.

A recurrent temptation of enthusiasts and reformers
is to appropriate this way of acting of the Lord, to say,
"I act and say these things because I act and say these
things. And that's all there is to it!" Christ, for the Christian, is the only one who can take such a stance. Everyone after him must be measured and be guided by the
witness to Christ's life as mediated to us by the first Christians. The reluctance of a person to be guided by any
tradition or norm outside himself is a sure sign of enthusiasm gone astray. It is a principle at the heart of Christianity that a message has been given to us and to which we

must conform. Jesus is the new Moses, and Christians are not expecting another one.

There is another point of instruction for us which flows from this little community around the Lord. It was a theme in the ascetical teaching of Clement of Alexandria, and the history of religious communities in the Church has proved its validity. It is this: The believer must be guided in his life of God by the living example of another person. The monks of the desert used to tell novices, "Just do what I do." People used to come to the Hasidic masters not to hear their words but simply to watch them tie their shoes!

Is it not true that often, when one finds a dynamic Christian community, there is a dynamic person at the center? We think immediately of the first followers of the founders and foundresses of religious orders and lay groups in the history of the Church. They were attracted by a living example of the gospel. St. Anthony literally drew hundreds of people into the monastic way of life by the power of his life. Communities, and eventually a whole way of life in the Church for centuries to come, were formed around his living example. In such cases the power of an individual's example becomes a pervasive and guiding influence on the community, combining, in some analogous way, office and charisma as in the case of Christ himself.

Many of the problems and causes of superficial Christian living are due to the fact that there are no living examples around. This may seem a commonplace to say, but we often fail to recognize that when living examples are not around, we take our signals from more abstract and therefore often more legalistic sources. When there are no living examples around, we must rely on traditions and constitutions and codes, often drawn up by founders and foundresses, but eventually becoming dead letters instead of living expressions of the Spirit. Having mere documents as our guides is the price we pay for not becoming living incarnations of the gospel ourselves.

Another theological concept which is important for our understanding of the relationship between office and charisma has to do with the notion of the proclamation of the gospel as a principle of authority in the community. This is extremely important, but rather an elusive concept to describe. A couple of examples from St. Paul may help.

St. Paul does not simply give orders or create norms which are to be followed and obeyed. It is true that he gives his opinions on matters submitted to him for comment; it is also true that he, at times, appears to be giving strict rules for everyone to follow. But at a deeper level, Paul sees the power of the gospel itself as the final argument.

The apostles were primarily missionaries. Preaching is of the essence of their apostolate. When difficulties arise in the communities, Paul's approach is one of proclaiming to them again the original message. His conception of "how to keep order" in the community is bound up with the notion of "reminding people" of the gospel. "For the mark of every admonition is 'remembrance,' recollection of the basic indicative of that divine election of which the congregation have in Christ been made partakers."[6] Paul's concept of the apostolate is entirely one of proclamation, not of organization.[7]

When Paul heard about the various factions forming in Corinth, he did not take the approach that "he had expressly forbidden such factions and groups from forming." No, he proclaimed for them again the gospel, that it was Christ who had died for them. How then can they go around following other personages? Did Peter or Paul or Apollos die for them?

In his approach to moral questions, for example, the problem of prostitution, he does not appeal to moral laws he has laid down. He *reminds* them again of their oneness in Christ: If their bodies are joined to the Lord, how can they give them over to immoral practices? It is unthinkable! This general attitude is well expressed in the opening admonition to the Galatians: "I am amazed that you are so readily deserting for a different gospel him who called you by the grace of Christ" (1:6).

Or, we may take a more domestic example. When a father comes home from work and discovers that the children have misbehaved, he can take one of several approaches. He can point to the rules of the house which he has made and which they have broken. He can also "remind" them of many things he and their mother have done for them, how he and she work hard all day for them, etc., and "is this the thanks we get?"

Paul's approach was something like this. He does not point to rules, but to what Christ has done for them. Let the impact of Christ's love rule their lives. "It is a matter of continuance in the basic attitude of the new redeemed being."[8] Spiritual authority consists in constant reminding, encouragement, and admonition.[9] Then there follows a most beautiful sentence which all those in positions of authority might well take as their motto: "The preaching of the gospel is the only thing which calls to life the Spirit through which the congregation can become what it is."[10]

I think we can begin to sense here a root cause of many problems in a Christian community. The power of the gospel proclamation was and is meant to be the basic formative agent. What happens if there is no one in the community who understands the gospel and is present to proclaim it powerfully? What happens is that the community "descends" to other ways of keeping people in order. Appeal is made to rules and regulations. To be sure, there is something of the gospel present. Motives will be guided by love and so forth, but it often is a strange mixture of rules being observed through love, instead of love constantly refashioning the rules. It is the power of the gospel's proclamation which creates order in hearts and minds. Rules (which always must have a place) will be in the secondary place where they belong.

Consciously or unconsciously, then, Christian communities often take as models of organization patterns from the political or business world around them. Neither is this necessarily a bad thing, as long as the models themselves do not become "sacred" and are not given an immovable status. It is evident that the early missionaries were not so much concerned with establishing communities (though this was definitely part of their mission) as with proclaiming the gospel. So far as the development and organization of these communities were concerned, they were left more or less to their own devices.

There were a variety of organizational patterns in operation. This was so because "the community [was] not viewed or understood as a sociological entity, and the Spirit which governs it does not act within the framework of a particular church order or constitution."[11] "It is love . . . which creates in her a paradoxical form of order diametrically opposed to all natural systems of organization."[12] "Christians have in very fact died to the old 'human nature,' and thus also to the old ideas of status and social order."[13]

These principles contain at least two lessons for us.

First, that we must beware of using secular models of organization for Christian communities which are set up by and demand for their functioning principles quite other than love in Christ. The Spirit of Love is not limited to organizational lines set up by Christians. He may wish to speak through a new or "uninformed" member who does not belong to the "board." People may have gifts which ought to be used now, without waiting for their turn in the "line of seniority," or until they "come up through the ranks." How many gifts have been left untapped because their use did not fit in with the system of organization? How many talents are neglected because the love operative in the community is neither clear-sighted nor humble enough to recognize them?

The second lesson is that a variety of structures are possible. It is not a matter of doing away with structure but of giving the Spirit credit for being able to inspire a variety of patterns in keeping with the needs and abilities of the members of the community.

From the very early days of the apostles, the communities are marked by a definite shape and structure—but these vary. Structure was fluid and elastic enough to allow the Spirit to breathe through its members. There is no theological reason why religious communities cannot allow for a variety of organizational patterns and for all kinds of exceptions to the patterns that are established. The discerning sensitivity of love must be the final criterion of how the gifts of each are used in practical affairs.

Paul is the exemplar of the builder of community who allows the most freedom for the Spirit. As was stated above, this does not mean that his is *the* model, or that the description of his communities which can be gleaned from his two letters to the Corinthians is complete. We will see, I think, that the picture there is *not* complete.

There are some very significant principles, however, discernible in Paul's approach, which must form part of our total approach. Paul never addresses himself (i.e., in the letters actually written by Paul) to one single person or group as responsible for the whole well-being of the others. As a matter of principle, there is no "ruling class" in the congregation. Even the "spiritual men are not thought of, at least by Paul, at any rate, as a 'pneumatic aristocracy.' "[14] Ultimate decisions are always left to the congregation. Relationships of position in the community arise spontaneously and do not allow of legal definitions. Ministries do not rest on human organizational planning but on the gift of the Spirit. Neither is there a sharp dividing line between spiritual and practical services. When new ministries arise they do not establish new systems but are incorporated into the prevailing outlook. "The most striking feature is the complete lack of any legal system, and the exclusion on principle of all formal authority within the congregation."[15]

It is no wonder that enthusiastic movements of all kinds have appealed to Paul. And if they only confine themselves to letters like Corinthians, they are perfectly right. There was a freedom and elasticity about his communities that was quite phenomenal. The problem lies in taking these communities as models and simply attempting to imitate them centuries later. We will see shortly that factors arose subsequent to the very early years which demanded a different approach to community organization. Some of these factors might rightly be viewed as degenerations. But others were part and parcel of the historical distancing from origins. They are necessary, unavoidable, and perfectly valid.

The most obvious and important of such latter factors was the whole notion of tradition, and the need to safeguard the apostolic witness:

> The elders and governing bishops would never have been able to win that decisive recognition of their dignity and authority which they did had not something in their position corresponded from the start to the religious nature of the Church and its spiritual needs . . . it is the concept of tradition.[16]

There is something very profound in this statement for the whole understanding of the development of Christian communities. The freedom of the Spirit and the ability to be open to his gifts is *not enough*. Some new element must enter in to preserve the original message. Some kind of continuity with the past is demanded. It is precisely the elders and the people learned in the tradition who provide this stability.

Paul, in the letters actually written by him, is silent on the notion of office because "it is plain that he simply has not reckoned with the possibility that there might be a need for special measures to safeguard the fundamental apostolic witness."[17] "What he is not acquainted with, and therefore has not yet allowed for, is a gradual, almost imperceptible drying up and disappearance of that tradition which he sees as something so unitary and translucent. . . ."[18] Given his "proclamation approach" to the formation of communities, it is no wonder that we do not find an office-oriented community in Paul's writings.

A superficial reading of scripture and subsequent Church history might lead one to look upon this development of office to preserve tradition as an aberration, or even as a sign of weakness, or as being "less free in the

Spirit." Von Campenhausen insists that it was not:

> It would be simply perverse, however, to see this development as something like a deliberate rejection of the sovereignty of the Spirit in favor of "mere" tradition. In the period we are considering, both these things go together; belief in the Spirit as something alien to tradition, something encountered only in direct religious experience, is no part of early Christianity, but only of the later Middle Ages and of modern times. The truth is that on all sides sacred tradition is sought out, discovered, and prized.[19]

In our own day we are witnessing the springing up of various charismatic and Christian groups. In some of them there is the ever-present temptation mentioned above, the temptation to "start from scratch" as far as building a Christian community. "Prayer, good will, openness to the Spirit, and the scriptures are all that is necessary." This drive to "return to origins" and to the simple, unstructured format of (most often Paul's) early Christian community where the Spirit is free to blow as he wills is most appealing. It does not, however, square with the real facts.

Very early the notion and reality of tradition and the interconnectedness of communities began to function. Even Paul's congregations "are not independent guilds of initiates, absorbed in themselves and their own religious life. They are all involved with one another."[20] Later on there is always the thread of continuity with the past, with tradition, preserved by the elders and those who have gone before. Again, the rejection of the reality of tradition and therefore of a group of people especially entrusted to hand on this tradition cannot be justified by an appeal to limited sections of the New Testament.

Another modern misconception is that there was always some kind of major tension between officeholders and free men of the Spirit. However, on into the second century, there is much evidence of the matter-of-fact *coexistence* of these two groups. Both of them are subordinate to the apostolic testimony. This tension *does* become acute in the encounter with Montanism, with unfortunate effects for the Church.

Paul and the early Christian elders did not seem to find in charismatic people the real enemies of the gospel. Yes, Paul had warnings for them and had to restrain them, but for Paul the true opponents of the gospel are in the camp of the legalists. We often forget that legalism is a kind of practical heresy. It too can lead to doctrinal aberrations, as when it tends to deny individuals in the community the exercise of their gifts. It seems that in Paul's mind he was much more afraid of legalism than enthusiastic extremists.

As far as Paul's principles of discernment are concerned, they were basically of two kinds: submission to the judgment of the community, and remaining united in love. This is to say that when prophecies or utterances came forth from the community, the marks of genuineness were whether or not the person would submit his message to the judgment of the community, and whether it fostered love and peace rather than strife and contention. Fraudulent men of the Spirit evade such tests, as do sometimes those who hold office. In Paul's mind it is only in the assembly of the Spirit-filled community where aberrations of both become apparent.

It may be countered that Paul also knew of tradition as a guide, for he speaks of the teaching that he himself received and passed on to the Corinthians as regards the Eucharist (1 Cor 11:23). It is true, "Paul too knows of a tradition which is no less a primary constituent of the Church than is the Spirit. It is simply that he drew no conclusions from it for the life of the community. The next generations were unable to maintain this position."[21]

Finally, we come to consider some of the factors which played a major role in the development of structures which differed from the structures of Paul's early communities. These factors, I believe, are important for anyone involved in the continued growth of Christian communities.

Basically, the structures become more "official," which need not have an adverse connotation. Office, in the second generation, was thought of as spiritual, and is not bound up, at least in the early decades, with legalism as such. Among the factors leading to this more official structuring, Von Campenhausen lists four: 1) the increasing remoteness of the Church's beginnings; 2) the emergence of heretical deviations; 3) the growth in numbers; 4) the flagging zeal in the congregation. We have already said something about the first point, namely, that the notion of tradition develops as time goes on, and that this was an unavoidable and a valid development. A group of people help to preserve the tradition. Such a group is naturally called upon to safeguard and protect the tradition in the face of opposing and heretical views. We would like to close this chapter by making a few remarks about the third and fourth points, and their relevance for Christian communities today.

Paul's concept of community was that each person had some gift to contribute and that by the harmonious blending of these gifts the body of Christ was built up. His concern was to "relativize and refract all authority to ensure the freedom of the congregation and their direct contact with Christ."[22] In our author's study a growing pattern is in evidence. As numbers grow, people become more passive. As people become more passive, gifts become less evident. As gifts become less evident, guidance of the community becomes more and more confined to a few people. In this situation, certain leaders must take over and guide the community—if not "must" at least this is what happens. One of the factors involved in the growth of office then is this growth in numbers and the lessening of the gifts.

By the time of the pastoral epistles (which according to most exegetes were not written by Paul), letters are now addressed to individuals who are in charge of stopping people from teaching false doctrine (1 Tm 1:3). Responsibility now for holding fast to tradition is vested in individual leaders. Charisma becomes a sacramental act which imparts grace appropriate to the office. "Do not neglect the spiritual gift that is in you, which was given to you when the prophets spoke and the elders laid their hands on you" (1 Tm 4:14). The presence here of prophets and elders working together should be noted.

It is a commonplace that where numbers grow, passivity grows. Yet, this fact has too little been taken into consideration where Christian communities are concerned. Size actually changes the approach to the Christ-life, often for the worse. The stepchild of large numbers is frequently passivity, an immature waiting to be served rather than the taking of one's rightful place of service in the community.

That flagging zeal helps lead to a one-sided concept of office needs no elaboration. There will always be people around who are willing to relieve others of the burden of freedom and responsibility. The desire to be safe instead of free is deep within us.

We experience the need for both permanence and

change in our lives. In societies and communities, this tension is experienced in terms of order as the condition for excellence and order as stifling the freshness of living. The philosopher A. N. Whitehead reminds us that both novelty (which for our purposes we can equate with charisma) and order (office) are necessary for life:

> But the two elements must not really be disjoined. It belongs to the goodness of the world, that its settled order should deal tenderly with the faint discordant light of the dawn of another age. Also, order, as it sinks into the background before new conditions, has its requirements. The old dominance should be transformed into the firm foundations, upon which new feelings arise, drawing their intensities from the delicacies of contrast between system and freshness.[23]

Generally speaking, we think of charisma as the element of newness, freshness and novelty; office concerns itself mostly with permanence and the settled order necessary for excellence. Of course, officeholders ought to be creative, and charismatic people ought to be concerned with tradition and order. Sometimes they are. We know that in both theory and practice there is no reason why both office and charisma cannot be sensitive to the basic orientation of the other. One would think that the officeholder who is truly in the Spirit would know how "to deal tenderly with the faint discordant light of the dawn of another age." Likewise, the charismatic who is truly in the Spirit should know how to transform old dominances into new firm foundations without giving the impression of trying to destroy them altogether. Thus will the balance between freshness and system be kept, to the glory of the Lord.

Chapter 6

Have Your Answer Ready for People Who Ask You for the Reason
— 1 Pt 3:15

The object of this chapter is twofold: 1) to be an exercise for enthusiasts in dispassionate thinking, and 2) to try and shed a little light, from the perspective of the charismatic renewal, on the problems involved with demythologizing.

There are many obstacles to the right channeling of enthusiasm. One of them is an inability or reluctance to think dispassionately about objections people raise to things which seem to strike at the heart of our faith. We are bound up intensely with our faith commitments and beliefs. Add to this a certain amount of enthusiasm, and some people may find it almost impossible to discuss objectively touchy points of scripture or theology.

For some people, the name of Rudolf Bultmann engenders just such irrational and violent reactions. Few people have taken the time to read him; most connect his name with "something about calling everything in the bible a myth." If, after reading him, we still disagree, we should be open enough to try and see his contribution to modern biblical studies. It would be undesirable for those in the churches today to try and return to an uncritical and unreflective approach to the bible — a kind of new fundamentalism, only now more enthusiastic!

100

In the present chapter we would like to briefly examine certain aspects of Bultmann's thought about demythologizing. At the end of our inquiry it may well be that we disagree with him; it may also happen that we will discover something valuable for our understanding of the bible. In any case, we may come to appreciate a bit more the gift of our intellects, and how it can help channel our enthusiasm in the right directions.

A curious phenomenon in this whole area of God language is continuing in the churches of today, and it is being highlighted by what is happening in the charismatic renewal. What the demythologizers said would no longer be possible is continuing to happen, and in the charismatic renewal in a more intensive way than ever. They said that modern man could no longer relate to the symbolism of the bible because that symbolism was built on a world view which modern man no longer shares:

> It is impossible to use electric lights and the wireless and to avail ourselves of modern medical and surgical discoveries, and at the same time to believe in the New Testament world of spirits and miracles. We may think we can manage it in our own lives, but to expect others to do so is to make the Christian faith unintelligible and unacceptable to the modern world.[1]

However, many people in the Church today—including those who have been through Teilhard, Baum, Evely, Dewart and some of the death of God theologians—still use biblical terminology such as Savior, kingdom, heaven, hell, devil and angel, and apparently relate to such notions quite well.

Or do they? Are these word symbols from another

cosmology (in Bultmann's view) really all that meaningful, or is modern man, out of sheer desperation, holding on to and/or returning to a pre-19th-century, fundamentalist mentality? Is modern man, the one who still uses these words, schizophrenically disregarding his modern mind set and in some blind, head-in-the-sand fashion accepting a biblical view of the universe simply to survive? Is what Bultmann feared really happening after all?

> Of course, there are today some survivals and re-vivals of primitive thinking and superstition. But the preaching of the Church would make a disastrous mistake if it looked to such revivals and conformed to them.[2]

It is presumed that the reader is acquainted suffi-ciently with modern biblical studies to know that Bultmann is one of the great theological thinkers of the 20th century. One does not have to agree with everything a person says before recognizing greatness. And, if the above quotations were the reader's first encounter with Bultmann, he would not likely become No. 1 on the reading list of those involved in the charismatic renewal!

What follows is not so much a debate with Bultmann (which would be rather presumptuous for the present author), as the posing of certain questions in the light of the charismatic renewal. It is not being implied that it is only now, through the charismatic renewal, that we have clear insights into what we consider inadequate or wrong with Bultmann's views. The point is that the charismatic renewal has brought into sharper focus some of the issues. After all, Bultmann himself says that "your own relation to the subject-matter prompts the question you bring to the text and elicits the answers you obtain from the text."[3] The charismatic renewal has changed many people's "relation to the subject matter," that is, to the events described in the scriptures. For someone unfamiliar with Bultmann all of what has been said so far must seem quite mystifying. It is time to get to the problem.

It is necessary, first of all, to get a brief but as clear a picture as possible of Bultmann's position. We will confine ourselves, for the most part, to his book, *Jesus Christ and Mythology,* which was billed as a "clarification of his revolutionary interpretation of New Testament materials." Bultmann is often clearer than his interpreters. With few exceptions, we will confine ourselves to his own words.

What are some of the things in the New Testament which Bultmann considers mythological?

> Just as mythological are the presuppositions of the expectation of the Kingdom of God, namely, the theory that the world, although created by God, is ruled by the devil, Satan, and that his army, the demons, is the cause of all evil, sin, and disease. The whole conception of the world which is presupposed in the preaching of Jesus as in the New Testament generally is mythological; i.e., the conception of the world as being structured in three stories, heaven, hell, and earth; the conception of the intervention of supernatural powers in the course of events; the conception of miracles, especially the conception of the intervention of supernatural powers in the inner life of the soul, the conception that men can be tempted and corrupted by the devil and possessed by evil spirits.[4]

The preaching of the New Testament proclaims Jesus

Christ, not only his preaching of the Kingdom of God but first of all his person, which was mythologized from the very beginning of earliest Christianity.[5]

His person is viewed in the light of mythology when he is said to have been begotten of the Holy Spirit and born of a virgin. . . .[6]

Many other examples of myth are given, but these will suffice.

This much is clear. These are myths in the New Testament according to Bultmann. But what, in his view, is a myth?

. . . the real purpose of myth is not to present an objective picture of the world as it is, but to express man's understanding of himself in the world in which he lives. Myth should be interpreted not cosmologically, but anthropologically, or better still, existentially.

He [the biblical writer] speaks of the other world in terms of this world, and of the gods in terms derived from human life. . . .

myth . . . with its apparent claim to objective validity. The real purpose of myth is to speak of a transcendent power which controls the world and man, but that purpose is impeded and obscured by the terms in which it is expressed.[7]

A simple and obvious example of what Bultmann means here is the way the bible speaks about the transcendence of God. He is "up in heaven." Here the bible uses a cosmological category—"up"—to express what in reality is a dimension of man's understanding of his relationship to God, namely, that God is "Other" or "totally Other." To speak of God as "up" is to obscure the reality of what is meant.

A similar example would be the phrase that Christ "descended into hell." The people of the bible believed in a three-story universe. The descent of Christ into hell undoubtedly expresses an aspect of Christ's saving mission, but that meaning is obscured, according to Bultmann, by using spatial images to express it. If people today simply nod their heads in assent (Bultmann questions whether this is even possible anymore) to this cosmological statement, they will miss the deeper meaning of what it was meant to say.

This leads us to our next point: What exactly is demythologizing in Bultmann's view? "Demythologizing is an hermeneutic method, that is, a method of interpretation, of exegesis."[8] "This method of interpretation of the New Testament which tries to recover the deeper meaning behind the mythological conceptions I call demythologizing —an unsatisfactory word, to be sure. Its aim is not to eliminate the mythological statements but to interpret them."[9]

Finally, it is not a matter of trying to pick and choose what in the New Testament is mythology and what is not. "Whatever else may be true, we cannot save the kerygma by selecting some of its features and subtracting others, and thus reduce the amount of mythology in it. And if we once start subtracting from the kerygma, where are we to draw the line? The mythical view of the world must be accepted or rejected in its entirety."[10]

My purpose is to try and approach the demythologizing problem in the specific light of the charismatic renewal, using some of Bultmann's own criteria for working out the difficulties. If the conclusions are not new, what may be new is using the occurrences in the renewal as a point of reference. Neither does this mean that the Catholic Church needed the charismatic renewal to come along before she was able to see clearly in this matter. No. It's just that the charismatic renewal has brought into clearer focus, it seems to me, a specific approach to the problems involved.

Bultmann is quite clear on the point that you cannot approach any text, whether of the bible or any book whatever, without presuppositions of some kind. "Exegesis is always based on principles and conceptions which guide exegesis as presuppositions, although interpreters are often not aware of this fact."[11] "Every interpreter brings with him certain conceptions, perhaps idealistic or psychological, as presuppositions of his exegesis. . . . But the question arises, which conceptions are right and adequate?"[12] "The resulting or corresponding presupposition of exegesis is that you do have a relation to the subject-matter . . . about which you interrogate a given text. I call this relation, the 'life-relation.' "[13]

Hand the same book, any book, to ten different people, and you will get ten different interpretations. Depending on their backgrounds, they will each select, almost unknowingly, what is of most importance to them, what is more understandable to them, etc. In the case of the bible, depending on the mental selectors, each will look for and be struck by different things. If you are a peacenik, you will see only the Man of Peace in the gospel and not his sternness. If you do not believe in private prayer, you will miss his nights on the mountain. If you are a death-of-God

theologian, you will explain away Christ's consciousness of
his Father. If you are a humanist you will see the Father
as Jesus' way of speaking about ultimate "Value" so that
his contemporaries could understand him. "Now the question arises as to which is the adequate method, which are
the adequate conceptions? And also, which is the relation,
the life-relation. . . .?"[14]

There are many dimensions to this "life-relation."
Bultmann himself relies heavily on the scientific world view
and aspects of existential philosophy to compose his proper
life-relation. Enough pros and cons have been written
about that. What I would like to do is simply expand a
a little on the notion that *what is happening in the charismatic renewal is an element of some modern men's life situation, life-relation, that must be taken into account in the
exegesis of the New Testament today.* "Life-relation" ought
not refer only to one's philosophical and mental categories,
but *to the whole of one's Christian life experience in the
Church today.*

It is a key point of Bultmann's own theology that "he
believes revelation to be an event which occurs exclusively
here and now, in the preaching of the Church, an event in
which God asks questions of man."[15] Thus, since we are
challenged by God, our focus when reading the bible ought
to be "to hear what the bible has to say for our actual
present, to hear what is the truth about our life and about
our goal."[16]

But the crux of this problem seems to be: What does
the Church preach? If men are questioned by God through
the preaching of the Church, where does the Church get
the conceptions for the posing of the questions? My answer
would be: from her present experience of the total mystery
of Christ. As she moves through history she acquires vari-

ations in the way she presents Christ to the world. Does not the preaching of the Church flow out of her present understanding and experience of the Christian message?

If this is so, my main point would be that people involved in the charismatic renewal (but not confined to them, of course) are experiencing as objectively real—as *cosmological*—some of the happenings in the bible which Bultmann claims are mythological, that is, not cosmological. I refer to two things, specifically, physical healings, and the exorcism of evil spirits. These events are happening now just as they happened in the accounts of the bible.

This is not the place to try and prove or witness to strict demythologizers that such things actually are happening. It will simply be stated that testimonies are growing daily of people who have witnessed both of these things.[17] These experiences are now for many people new elements in their "life-relation" to the gospels. Because they have actually experienced such things, they also can do no less than accept them as cosmological in the strict sense in the gospel stories as well.

People who believe in the charismatic renewal (but not only these) have, therefore, something to say to the demythologizers. They are saying that from their present "life-relation," their present experience of miracles of healing and the reality of evil spirits, the language of the bible is *not of one whole,* and that we cannot avoid the "subtracting" that Bultmann himself seemed to fear. The events narrated in the gospels are not that simple, and it may be true to say that, for some of them, it will always have to be a matter of faith whether one accepts them as objectively true or not.

A case in point is the Virgin birth. It is not a clear instance of the existential translated into the cosmological (e.g., "up" to express transcendence), nor is it of such a nature as to be experienced again in our present Christian lives (e.g., miracles of healing).

Father Raymond Brown, S.S., one of our best American scripture scholars, after a long study of the question, concludes: "My judgment, in conclusion, is that the totality of the scientifically controllable evidence leaves an unresolved problem."[18]

In other words, even from a *strictly scientific point of view,* it cannot be shown that everything is myth in Bultmann's sense. Thus there are at least three levels of language in the bible, in relation to us. There is the 1) obviously cosmological, 2) the objectively real, and 3) the unclear areas (and these latter must be decided by criteria such as tradition and the teaching of the Church).

Bultmann's genius lies in the fact that he has reminded us that every statement about the mystery of Christ must be translated into existential and meaningful terms so as to challenge us—so that God may question us—here and now. It is a matter of not treating as *mere facts* here and now even those realities we believe objectively real in the scriptures. If we do that, these realities become rather *pieces of information* which do not serve as meeting grounds with the Lord.

Bultmann points out that the kind of demythologizing he deems necessary was already begun by some of the New Testament writers themselves. If realities such as "judgment" and "eternal life" and "anti-Christ" were thought to be eschatological events, John points out that the reality of these things is happening now. With regard to judgment: "And this *is* the judgment, that the light has come into the world, and men loved darkness rather than the light. . . ." (Jn 3:19). In a real sense, judgment is *now.*

With regard to eternal life: "He who believes in the Son *has* eternal life. . . ." (Jn 3:36). Whatever heaven or eternal life may mean after death, it is also a present reality in which we are presently involved.

Or as regards the anti-Christ:

> In Jewish eschatological expectations we find that the figure of the anti-Christ is a thoroughly mythological figure as it is described, for example, in II Thes (2:7-12). In John (1 Jn 2:22) false teachers play the role of this mythological figure. These examples show, it seems to me, that demythologizing has its beginning in the New Testament itself, and therefore our task of demythologizing today is justified.[19]

In our day-to-day life with God, in the constant dialogue and decision-making that ensues between us and the world around us, who is or what is anti-Christ? St. John says it is anyone who denies that Jesus Christ has come in the flesh. To merely make the anti-Christ an eschatological figure is to miss the existential meaning of anti-Christ in the present.

There is a way, then, of accepting as objective facts heaven, hell and even the resurrection of Christ, and at the same time to rob them of their salvational power. "Many questions asked about the Church's teaching on eternal life presuppose a desire for total objectivization, and to reply to them might satisfy people's curiosity for a time but would ultimately weaken the salvational power of Christ's message."[20]

Many people believe that Jesus objectively rose from the dead. But the meaning of that has little or no effect on their relationship with God. That Jesus is alive means that he has conquered everything that separated us from the Father, that he is now Lord and able to draw us to him. Bultmann's point would be that if one does not have these latter points operative in one's life with God, in reality they do not believe in the resurrection at all. They have objectivized what should be an existential truth of their lives with God. "The task of demythologizing has no other purpose but to make clear the call of the Word of God. It will interpret the scripture, asking for deeper meaning of mythological conceptions and freeing the Word of God from a bygone world view."[21]

Much popular theological writing in the Church today is exciting precisely because it has translated objective truths of the bible into existential truths for us now.

One example that comes to mind from memory is from Anthony Padovano's book, *Dawn Without Darkness*. It is in the section on Easter, and he writes: "Jesus easters in us whenever people come home to themselves in our presence, and when they feel a little less hopeful because we are absent."

This may sound like poetry to some people, but hardly describing what the resurrection is all about. And yet, the deeper truth is that if somehow we are not people of hope to the extent that others can find in us a source of strength, then what does it mean to say that "nevertheless I believe that Jesus rose from the dead"? Religious wars have been fought over the objective truths of statements in the bible; and yet the meaning of those truths for the present was blotted out in bloodshed.

For those involved in the charismatic renewal, there is a danger of returning to a type of fundamentalism that fails to take into account the valid discoveries of modern scripture studies. Because scholars like Bultmann delve deeply into sacred things and come up with conclusions with which we do not agree, there is the tendency to disregard them entirely. In one sense, at least, Bultmann is quite right: There is no simple return, mentally, to the world of the New Testament. If we continue to use the terminology of the New Testament, as we must, our understanding of it will certainly be conditioned by the modern world in which we live. Some of that conditioning is good, and some harmful. Only an openness to the Spirit who speaks to us from many different quarters can keep us on the right road.

Thus, we must be open to him in the charismatic renewal, in the traditions of the churches, in faith, in what is valid in modern scripture studies, in what philosophers are saying, in prayer, and in honest dialogue with all men of good will. There are no simple, one-line answers available. A. N. Whitehead says that we neglect any area of truth at our own peril. Sooner or later there is a nemesis about such a rejection which catches up with us.

One of the liabilities of enthusiasm is a lack of critical judgment. Making intellectual distinctions ought not to be an obstacle to a living faith. We have been instructed by St. Peter's Epistle to "always have (an) answer ready for people who ask you the reason for the hope that you all have." A fear to use our minds may even be proof of a lack of faith. It is mostly for those heading back to a one-sided fundamentalism that this chapter was written.

If we are to be open to modern scripture studies, we would hope that scripture scholars would also be open to what the Spirit is doing in the lives of "little people." For scholars to disbelieve what many people are telling us is happening in their lives today is also not to be very objective. It would be equally disastrous for the Church if scholars were not open to realities which contradict what they are teaching.

No one, least of all Bultmann, wishes to remove the scandal of the gospel:

> He (Bultmann) agrees thoroughly with Barth and other neo-orthodox theologians that the gospel is strange, not just to modern man, but to all men. It is not to be accounted for in cultural terms, for it comes to man from outside all culture. This is just what myth, properly interpreted, safeguards.[22]

Many of us would agree that Bultmann has gone too far in his project. That is the present author's opinion also. Nonetheless, we do not want to lose the important contribution Bultmann has rendered to our understanding of the gospel message. Perhaps we need to pray for one another that we are all open to the Spirit so that together we might clearly hear what he is saying to the churches in our times.

Chapter 7

It Is Clear That There Are Serious Differences Among You

— 1 Cor 1:11

It did not take long for some of the early Christian communities to lose the vision of the importance of their oneness in Christ. They forgot that Christ had died that they might be one, and that everything was to be sacrificed to maintain this unity. Instead, splinter groups formed around the views and persons of Paul, Peter and Apollos. Unity was suffering because the members of the community were not bighearted or broad-minded enough to work out their differences in prayer, peace and mutual love.

To some people, the charismatic renewal has all the characteristics of another such faction. Unfortunately, the manner in which some people try and introduce others to it is overbearing and divisive. Especially has this been the case where the charismatic renewal enters a religious community of one type or another. Some such communities have literally been torn apart and fragmented by the manner in which people enthusiastic about the charismatic renewal have approached members of their communities. In the remarks which follow an attempt is made to point out the need for great delicacy and discernment on the part of those who feel called by the Lord in any way to be his instruments in introducing the charismatic renewal to their own or any particular already established Christian community.

Those involved in the renewal cannot help but believe that in some way the Lord is doing a new thing. On the other hand, the impression cannot be given (much less explicitly said) that up until this time the Spirit hasn't been acting at all! It is to help people approach a given community, keeping these two facts in perspective, that this chapter is devoted.

One of Father Kilian McDonnell's frequent themes is a plea not to "pentecostalize" the gifts of the Spirit. By this he means that we should not have so restricted and limited a view of the gifts of the Spirit that we fail to see them operative in ways and forms other than might be expressed at prayer meetings or described by pentecostal literature. One of the theological challenges here is to try and understand the heart and core of each gift, and then to recognize it however and wherever it may appear.

Can there be any doubt that especially in religious orders and in ecclesiastical institutions of all kinds, gifts such as wisdom, teaching, knowledge and prophecy have been operative in a variety of forms? In decisions concerning pastoral needs, in drawing up rules of life for the community, in the day-to-day adventure of living together, is not the finger of the Spirit of God evident? What tends to "turn people off" about a certain way of speaking and presenting the charismatic renewal is an implication, either direct or indirect, that what the Spirit is doing now is so entirely new that, in comparison, this or that community has, practically speaking, not been aware of the Spirit at all.

There certainly are new dimensions and elements in the charismatic renewal, but care must be exercised in defining this newness, whether it be one of essence, degree, or simply one of a different manifestation of an existing gift. The gift of tongues used in public prayer is certainly a new thing. Also, a kind of new level of consciousness of the Spirit's presence and an explicit awareness of his gifts, plus God's desire to pour out these gifts on his people. But already in these latter instances, we are perhaps talking of degrees of existing realities rather than entirely new phenomena. What is difficult for people, especially religious, to take, is to be told that up till now they have been "missing the boat" entirely.

Many communities in the Church are places of real faith and love. It may not be the exuberant and expressive faith and love of those who have been exposed to the charismatic renewal, but it is real nonetheless. Many people in these communities are already living out in a profound way the heart of everything St. Paul was trying to tell the Corinthians, i.e., that love is the greatest gift of all. They are mature lovers. Those who wish to bring the dimensions of the charismatic renewal to such people should beware of trying to measure love by the standards of spontaneous prayer, the gift of tongues, or the ability to openly and freely share their life in Christ. Often the inability to do these latter is attributable more to conditioning and years of particular life-styles. One can be a great lover without possessing the ability to express his or her life in Christ in an enthusiastic and charismatic way.

Having said this, namely, that real faith and love can be present in individuals and in a community without the specifically "charismatic" dimension, there is the temptation and tendency to conclude that therefore there is no real need for something like the charismatic renewal.

Those involved in the renewal would see this as a mistake in the other direction. To use an outdated theological label, it seems "morally certain" at this time to state that the charismatic renewal has reached a stage of legitimacy in the Church. There have been cautious but no completely negative statements about the charismatic renewal on the part of the Church hierarchy. On the contrary, public participation on the part of bishops and priests is increasing steadily. Just to quote one of many testimonies which could be cited. It is by Cardinal Suenens, the outstanding prelate of Malines-Brussels, Belgium, in a recent interview on the state of ecumenism:

> Ecumenism must be a constant concern of all Christians, whether or not theologians. The more a Christian accepts the gospel with the soul of a child, the more accessible he will be to the Lord's command "that they may all be one." This special openness to the Spirit, which is proper to all Christians, should be particularly treasured. This is why a certain number of "manifestations of the Spirit" which are taking place before our eyes among the people of God hold an extraordinary ecumenical importance for me.
>
> I am thinking in particular of the ecumenical contribution of the "charismatic renewal" which began in its Catholic form in America in 1966-67, and at this moment is spreading in Europe and elsewhere in an impressive way.[1]

If it is wrong to present the charismatic renewal as a sort of first introduction to the Holy Spirit, those who have adopted, for one reason or another, a standoffish attitude must in honesty ask themselves if they are perhaps not neglecting a providential movement of the Lord in our day.

A one-sided presentation by some people should not be used as an excuse for avoiding an honest attempt to understand what many are considering a valid impulse of the Spirit of God. It seems that no religious community—no individual in the Church—can avoid at this period of history an attempt to come to grips with the charismatic renewal and try to understand its possible meaning for a deeper life with Christ.

Another aspect of this meeting of the charismatic renewal and an existing community is to remember that the Spirit is present in both. Both are expressions of life in the Spirit. It is not a matter of two different spirits clashing—Paul with Apollos, Peter with Paul, the charismatic renewal with such and such an order or community. As with so many supposed conflicts and clashes, it is not a question of either/or but of *both/and*. People on either side of the clash are often so adamant precisely because they are convinced of the validity of what they see the Spirit doing. They may both be right. The Spirit is trying to teach both "sides" something new about life with the Lord.

The meeting is touchy because both expressions of life in the Spirit are valid and intense, and neither is going to be overly naive about the other. Thus, because both are inspired by the Spirit, the process of integration will not happen overnight—and no one should either wish or try to force it to happen thus. The charismatic renewal entering a religious community will be a gradual process, a mutual "feeling out of each other." Any attempt of the renewal to force itself upon a community would be a mistake. Each has something to learn from the other. For either position to assume a "know-it-all" attitude toward the other would be disastrous. Mutual modification and influence will take time—and ought to.

People who feel led to introduce the renewal to a particular community are often familiar, either through reading or personal contact, with charismatic communities such as at Ann Arbor, South Bend, or some of the others scattered around North America. There is a tendency to believe that every community must now be structured in the same way. The leaders involved in these charismatic communities are insistent that there should be no mere "copying" as far as community framework is concerned.

We live the life of a most creative and ingenious Spirit. He can make his gifts bear fruit in a variety of structures and patterns. Even in the early years of Christianity (as we have seen) there were a variety of structural patterns for community ranging from the system of elders in Jewish Christian groups to the more charismatically structured Pauline communities. The Spirit is not bound to particular organizational models. It is essential for his gifts to be operative, but this is an entirely different matter from the form and expression of those gifts in a community structure.

For one thing, communities such as Ann Arbor have arisen and been ordered "charismatically." From the very beginning they have been free to follow and discern the gifts of the Spirit in their members, and to organize their community according to the allotment of the Spirit's gifts to each. It is a beautiful work of the Lord to watch. But they have not had to deal with the problem of relating the Spirit's ordering of the community by his gifts with a religious rule or an ecclesiastical setup of one type or another.

Also, many of these communities deal with young people who have no religious formation similar to that which religious and priests have gone through. Therefore, the form and expression and the whole dynamic of how the gifts will operate and influence other communities will be different. The task and challenge of integrating the charismatic renewal into any specific community will be something that only that community can really do for itself. What is happening elsewhere can be instructive and helpful, but in the last resort each must recognize its uniqueness. Any attempt to simply duplicate what is happening in other communities would be unfortunate, not to say unreal.

There are thus many differences between "charismatic" communities and communities such as religious orders. Besides the differences mentioned, another is the regularity and close day-to-day contact in established religious communities. Because life is on this daily basis, the expressions of the Christ-life have a tendency to be more subdued— not necessarily less intense, but more subdued, more "low-key."

If you have ever made a cursillo weekend you know that, while it is a marvelous experience, one cannot live that enthusiastically—that "high"—every day. Thus, in religious communities, those who wish to introduce the charismatic dimension should be aware that the gifts may be and usually are present but in a much more subdued fashion.

Many charismatic communities are simply people from various walks of life who come together once, perhaps twice, a week. At these meetings there is much expression of the gifts and often a fair amount of enthusiasm. One reason for the enthusiasm is that this meeting is "all they have," in the sense that during the week they are often cut off from opportunities for such fellowship in the Lord.

This is not a criticism, merely an observation. The weekly prayer meeting is their opportunity to express themselves—a sort of high point of their week. It is not difficult to be enthusiastic and express the gifts in rather more overt ways once a week. It is another question what form the expression of the gifts would take if these people lived together daily. Such daily living is taking place in the "households" at Ann Arbor and elsewhere. It will be interesting to watch what forms the gifts assume after a few years of such community life.

For example, if people in a community are able to share their lives in Christ by talking together about his importance for them, if they can share the scriptures together, then certainly in such sharings the gifts of wisdom and knowledge and teaching are operating. That such gifts are expressed while eating together or while walking does not make them essentially different from the same gift being expressed at a prayer meeting in a certain stylized form. As remarked above, what is necessary is to try and understand the essence of each gift, and then be able to discern its presence in its various manifestations.

Most people have only a very limited number of contacts with the charismatic renewal. This means that many people, both those who welcome it and those who have many reservations about it, need to exercise a great deal of caution when discussing it. Those who are attracted to it may not have seen some of the questionable and dubious things that go on at some prayer meetings. Those who hold off from getting involved may have never been to a national convention and seen firsthand the tremendous impact the renewal is making in almost all areas of Church life. It is so important that neither group take a dogmatic attitude, since neither group is that well acquainted with all the pros and cons.

Much delicacy and tact are also needed because those

in religious orders—priests, sisters, brothers—are strong personalities. They have already formed very definite notions about what life in Christ—and their own life with him in particular—is all about. "Do you mean to tell me that after all these years of religious life I have been unaware of essential aspects of the Christian life?" is a question sometimes expressed, more often etched on their faces. Any attempt to force the charismatic renewal in this situation would be disastrous.

We know that the Spirit invites, not just in this matter but in all aspects of our coming to the Father. True love invites, and those who believe in the charismatic renewal will have the humility and patience to be good expressions of the inviting Spirit. Quiet witnessing, joy, respect for the freedom of others, the ability to discuss dispassionately the fears and apprehensions of those inquiring—these should be the characteristics of anyone really concerned with fostering the renewal. It would help greatly if people could sit down and intelligently discuss the matter without all sorts of emotional factors clouding the issues.

It would also be unfortunate if people who are really concerned about fostering the charismatic renewal gave the impression of forming a little clique within the community to which they belong. It is not so much a matter of those involved meeting to pray together. This is legitimate. Everything depends, however, on how people go about this.

Impressions of a "closed group" can be created in a hundred different ways, and we all are adept at doing so. It is up to those having the meetings to create an atmosphere of complete openness and a willingness to share. The community, for its part, must be bighearted enough to allow for a variety of faith and prayer needs on the part of its members. It is a sign of its own maturity in the

Spirit for the community to be able to live with a certain amount of diversity in the area of spiritualities. Within certain limits, a community must allow for the legitimate movements of the Spirit in the hearts of individuals. For the foreseeable future, there is no reason why religious communities cannot allow separate prayer meetings of a charismatic nature. One of the principal reasons for this is treated in Chapter 8 of this book.

Besides this prayer meeting, those interested in the renewal may also want to have what is known as a "core group" meeting. Its purpose is to discuss and pray over the many aspects of the renewal, to understand it better, and especially to try and understand how best to foster its integration into this particular community. Those unfavorable to the renewal may wish to label such meetings "divisive." They can *become* divisive, but only due to a lack of sensitivity on the part of either group.

More and more in the Church we must accustom ourselves to a good kind of pluralism in our approaches to God—in both theory and practice. If certain members of a given community find it beneficial for their growth in the Spirit to meet together for prayer and discussion, it would be a narrow-minded community indeed which could not find a place for them. People join religious communities to be able to follow the Spirit better. What a tragedy if members are not allowed to follow his legitimate leadings.

A charismatic core group meeting within a community has many advantages. It can be a source of spiritual growth for those who participate and, indirectly, another kind of witness in the Lord to other members of the community.

It is a positive benefit to see members of your community come together to pray, search the scriptures and share together their lives in Christ. This core group can become a sort of "hothouse" where new movements of the Spirit can be explored and perhaps presented to the larger community for its consideration. The structures of communities often prevent them from seeing clearly viable options in approaches to life together. The core group, because it is unstructured, might learn some valuable things about the formation of Christian community, which it could then share with the larger community for its judgment and evaluation. Members of the core group must remember that it is not the *whole* community, and that therefore its view and its judgment are rather limited.

A sure way to antagonize the larger community would be for the members of the core group to give the impression that this meeting of theirs is the most important event of the whole week! In practice, if not in theory, the impression can be given that this meeting is the high point of the week and that, if others only knew, it is from here that the real direction and inspiration of the community will come!

There is no doubt that the Lord wants to affect the whole community in certain ways through such a core group. The impression should not be given, however, that this meeting is now the hub around which everything else turns. Especially when the core group is small within a much larger community, it is simply a fact that the larger community *is* the community. According to the core group's own principles of discernment, it is this larger community's judgment which has the final say on matters of importance which affect the whole community.

This larger community may even judge that such a core group meeting is divisive. It would be vitally important then to desist from such meetings and wait for the Lord's own good time. Such acquiescence to the larger community's judgment can bear nothing but good fruit and be the surest sign of the Spirit's presence in the movement. The Lord has many ways of renewing hearts.

Another factor that might be operative in the reluctance of religious communities to accept the charismatic renewal is their very valid sensitivity that *love* is and must remain primary. For many years, members of these communities have been trained to regard with suspicion certain external manifestations of life in Christ. Now, it seems, the charismatic renewal is blessing an outward style of Christian spirituality which is simply the old externalism in new garb. "Can being able to pray out loud and clap your hands, can a new knowledge and conversation about the gifts of the Spirit really be the core of the Christian life? We were always taught that love was the heart of the gospel. Is the charismatic renewal another kind of trip? It seems so superficial."

People involved in the renewal would quite agree that there is something secondary (but not superficial) about it. They would agree that people can be real lovers of Christ without in any way being attracted to the particular spirituality of the charismatic movement. The Holy Spirit leads people by many different roads. The final criterion is certainly love, love of God and love of neighbor. In some real sense, the renewal is concerned with different ways of growing in and manifesting love. It is quite possible to be living a "charismatic" Christian life-style and not be growing in love at all.

It is believed, of course, that one can and ought to be growing in love through participation in the gifts of the Spirit. It is also believed that the gifts were meant precisely to aid the growth of love in a powerful way. Nevertheless, the impression cannot be conveyed that the charismatic renewal and those involved in it are now at a "deeper level" of love. Nor, to reverse the image, that it is a "higher form" of Christianity. Much of the charismatic renewal is concerned with new ways of expressing love and new insights as to how the Spirit is at work in us, leading us to the Father. It does not in any way guarantee that these new expressions are actually leading to deeper love, or that the new insights are culminating in the same deeper love.

Older religious would be among those most inclined to offer the above objections. They are quite valid. Sometimes the way people talk about the gifts, abuse them, and seem to place them above selfless love—not only in conversation but in their lives—gives abundant ground for such objections. It is no wonder that the renewal is then treated with reserve and suspicion. In comparison with mature love, the gifts *are* superficial.

> I may be able to speak the language of men and even of angels, but if I have not love, my speech is no more than a noisy gong or a clanging bell. I may have the gift of inspired preaching; I may have all knowledge and understand all secrets; I may have all the faith needed to move mountains—but if I have not love, I am nothing. I may give away everything I have, and even give up my body to be burned—but if I have not love, it does me no good (1 Cor 13:1-3).

We have all read these words of St. Paul many times. Those who are trying to introduce the renewal into religious houses must ask themselves if they really believe them. Many people who have been in religious communities for years are often mature in Christian love, although they may not be able to express it as openly as others—

as "charismatically." They have a fine sensitivity for what love is, and they will not be easily taken in by lesser gifts. We have all felt this criticism of the renewal in our hearts at times. It should not surprise us when we hear or feel it in others.

Everyone, however, should realize that the gifts are meant by the Lord to be means of growing in love and that, rightly understood and kept in perspective, they can be powerful means to that end. A valid sensitivity to the centrality of love should not be used as an excuse to neglect the gifts as legitimate means to attain this love.

A sign of maturity in persons and in a community would seem to be the ability to look honestly and squarely at the charismatic renewal, and try to appreciate whatever is good in it and of the Lord. If something like the charismatic renewal is capable of turning a whole community's life upside down, then it couldn't have been built on anything too solid in the first place. Perhaps it should have been turned upside down! A sign of spiritual health for both an individual and a community would be the ability to peacefully discern what is good in the renewal that could be used for spiritual growth.

A sign of spiritual sickness would be an abnormal fear that to "let the charismatic renewal into our community" is going to shake the whole foundation. If our lives are built on Christ the Rock, there is no danger. He promised that if we build our lives on his word, no wind or storm of any kind will be able to destroy our houses.

It is not easy to allow the Spirit to blow where he wills. Especially in the lives of institutions, the Spirit is very often made subordinate to structures and objective notions of how we ought to function. As institutions grow older, they acquire definite structures. Much freedom in the Spirit is needed for members to constantly appreciate that the Lord can speak and guide in ways other than these structures. The charismatic renewal is a providential instruction lesson by the Spirit concerning this fact.

To allow the charismatic renewal into a community is certainly to expose that community's structure to possible change and modification. (Nor should that be so threatening at this stage since the Spirit, working through the Second Vatican Council, has precipitated the same re-evaluations.) But any community built on the gospel and the Spirit of Jesus will have a strong faith that the same Spirit will continue to guide and enlighten and enable that community to discern in any contemporary movement what is of the Lord and beneficial for its spiritual growth.

Much needs to be written on the positive influence the charismatic renewal can have on an established religious community. But perhaps it is too premature for this. Few communities have 100 percent participation in the charismatic renewal. The present stage is still one of a mutual feeling out of each other, something akin to the stages of an early personal relationship. Neither person knows the other very well. Niceties are exchanged; many "games" are being played. Total openness is still a way off.

This chapter has been a plea for delicateness and sensitivity, the delicacy and sensitivity of true love in the Spirit. Further than that, it has been a plea for established communities to explore the charismatic renewal as a providential movement of the Spirit for our times. For the sake of the world for which Christ died, we cannot afford to neglect any inspiration of the Spirit, much less such a powerful one as the charismatic renewal.

At the present time there is absolutely no indication that the charismatic renewal is slowing up or abating in any way. Its particular spirituality and enthusiasm for the things of God continue to spread from person to person and from town to town. If at the end of the first chapter it was emphasized that each individual needs to question himself or herself concerning the challenge of the renewal, this chapter is a questioning and a challenge to already established communities: Have you, *as a community,* explored the possibilities for growth offered in the charismatic renewal?

The Roman Catholic Church has a genius for many things. One of them is its instinct to form communities. Did you ever stop to consider that the phenomenon of having religious communities, on any large scale, is almost exclusively a Catholic genius? The same pattern is happening again in the Catholic charismatic renewal.

At the 1973 National Service Conference at Ann Arbor, Rev. Vinson Synan of the Pentecostal Holiness Church had these remarks to make:

> It's been interesting for us, watching the Catholic renewal go through the same stages we went through 70 years ago. There is a certain naivete about it that's refreshing. But this strong sense of community is something we've never had. We are rejoicing, but we are amazed.[2]

When one considers the extraordinary variety of communities in the Catholic Church—communities of monks, priests, sisters, brothers, lay people, and now the charismatic communities of all shapes and sizes—we cannot but conclude that the attraction to form community is a peculiar inspiration of the Spirit within the Catholic communion. With our centuries of experience, we ought to be adept in helping people form community.

The charismatic renewal brings still another depth to enrich the community dimensions of the Church. If religious communities can be open to it, can explore what the Spirit is doing in and through it, then our communities can again become places of renewal, where people come to experience the presence of the Lord and see "how they love one another" (Acts 5:13).

Chapter 8

While They Were
Worshiping the Lord...

— *Acts 13:2*

Free-flowing group prayer meetings are taking place on
an unprecedented scale in the charismatic renewal. If one
had difficulty in believing in the Lord's instigation of the
charismatic renewal, surely the fact that thousands of
people come together each week to pray is in itself a
moral miracle of the first magnitude. But such group
prayer meetings have not been part of our recent traditional
history. How are we to understand them in relationship
to our other prayer and worship forms? This chapter tries
to shed some light on these questions. What is especially
being maintained here is that the reality of Christian group
prayer is being restored to the Church in all its fullness
through the convergence of various historical, theological
and now charismatic trends.

This may sound like quite a presumptuous statement.
Has not group prayer always been in the Church—the
Divine Office, the liturgical celebrations, the Eucharist
itself? These are various expressions of group prayer. What
is being contended is that the complexus of elements which
was present in the very early Christian gatherings was
gradually fragmented, and the remaining elements took on
several forms in the ongoing life of the Church. The basic

elements such as prayers, songs, the recitation of the psalms, homily and charismatic outpourings took on two forms, the Liturgy of the Word, to which the Eucharist was added on special occasions, and the Divine Office.[1] We are concerned here with exemplifying the historical route and restoration of group prayer in regard to the Divine Office; a similar trajectory and outcome could be traced in reference to the Liturgy of the Word, the fore-Mass.

More specifically, the point of this chapter is to show how, through various trends converging in our day, the unity and fullness of Christian group prayer is again being made possible. Historically we have come full circle from small gatherings of Christians in homes, on through the elaborations of the Office by the monks, and into the "private" recitation of the Office by priests and religious. The present stage of the Church's thinking about the Office is the desire to have all Christians pray her official prayer.

Theologically we have come from the concept of liturgy in Acts 13:1-2 where it meant simply Christians praying together, on through the notion of liturgy as "deputed prayer" and therefore somehow special, to the notion of the post-Vatican liturgical commission that when people come together in prayer true liturgy is taking place.

Charismatically, the Spirit is drawing more and more people into prayer groups and assisting them and teaching them to express some of the more spontaneous elements of Christian prayer. It is the purpose of this chapter to briefly trace these trends in history and show how the group prayer phenomenon of today is the flowering and renewal of authentic Christian prayer.

The group prayer of the early Christians, as far as its basic components are concerned, undoubtedly flowed from their experience of prayer in the synagogue. Even though the elements of the temple worship which were taken over into the synagogue are not easily discernible,[2] it seems that "the constant parts of the synagogue service were prayer, the reading of the lessons from the scriptures, followed, if a competent person was present, by a homily."[3]

Harnack rounds out our picture of early group prayer. After mentioning the elements we have just mentioned, he includes sacred song, then states: "In addition to these we have, as specifically Christian elements, the celebration of the Lord's supper, and the utterances of persons inspired by the Spirit. The latter manifestations, however, ceased in the course of the second century, and to some extent as early as its first half."[4] This latter point is quoted because, unlike expressions such as song, prayer, etc., which went through various manifestations, charismatic elements ceased altogether, at least as far as their appearance in public prayer services was concerned.[5]

We know that before the fourth century, the Christian people used to gather in churches for the daily singing of psalms and prayer (e.g., the virgins and ascetics in the Church of Jerusalem). With the flight to the desert and the beginnings of monasticism, there develops the Divine Office or *Opus Dei*. A kind of group prayer which up to about the third century had been rather private though corporate—and rather simple as to its form—with the advent of monasteries takes on a growing elaborateness and begins to assume a quasi-official status. The coming together for prayer of the ordinary Christian outside specifically eucharistic celebrations disappears from the scene. When, in the sixth century, the monks moved into the towns and closer to churches and basilicas, the Divine Office had become the Church's public prayer, the province of monks and canons.

The Benedictines, especially, spread the Office wherever they went. Over the centuries the elaboration of this form of prayer continued with the addition of offices for the saints, for the dead and for Our Lady. By then a number of books were needed to celebrate the Office, and by the 12th century various attempts were made to consolidate these books into "breviaries" or "little books."

All during these centuries popular devotions of many types were springing up. One reason is that the official prayer of the Church was no longer accessible to or understandable by the simple lay person. Finally, by the 16th century, due to the breakup of the corporate concept of the Church, even public recitation of the Office by the clergy became an exception. It had become a complex form of prayer to be recited in private by priests and religious. For many people, the *Opus Dei* had become an *onus!*

Reforms were attempted by Trent, by Pius X, and by Pius XII. The latter wrote in *Mediator Dei* (1947): "In an earlier age these canonical hours were attended by many of the faithful, but this gradually ceased, and . . . their recitation at present is the duty only of the clergy and of religious. The laity have no obligation in this matter" (Part III, No. 150).

What originally began as the common prayer of the people of God, still, in 1947, is not restored to them. It is still the concern of a specialized group. Most of the laity in the Church have never in their lives recited even one hour of the Divine Office, the prayer of the Church.

Postconciliar documents, however, are finally returning to the concept of the Office as the prayer of all the faithful. The titles of both the Canadian and American Interim Breviaries express this. The former is called *The*

Prayer of the Church and the latter *The Prayer of Christians.* This is perfectly in keeping with the intention of the reform as expressed by A. Bugnini, Secretary of the Sacred Congregation for Divine Worship, in his introduction to the *General Instruction on the Liturgy of the Hours* (the new official title for the "Divine Office"): "The awareness of the Liturgy of the Hours as something belonging essentially to the whole Church has, regrettably, hardly been in evidence for many centuries. The liturgical reform seeks to restore the Liturgy of the Hours as a celebration of the whole Church community, the holy people of God. This is the purpose of the renewed Liturgy of the Hours."[6] The same thought is found in Pope Paul's Apostolic Constitution *Laudis Canticum:* ". . . the prayers of the hours are proposed to all the faithful . . . to those who are not obliged by law to recite them."[7]

Officially, then, we have returned to the notion of the Church's traditional group prayer as a prayer to be celebrated by all the people. But is this practical? Is it possible? We shall return to these questions a bit later.

The theological underpinnings behind the historical development just traced are also important to consider. In the course of the centuries the notion of liturgy, at least as far as the Divine Office was concerned, became a special kind of prayer, the celebration of which was somehow raised to a special level precisely by being delegated. The remnants of this approach are noticeable in the above quotation from the Pope—"to those who are not obligated by law to recite them"—although a new understanding now accompanies such statements.

While there is validity to the notion of obliging certain members to forms of prayer as a way of sacramentalizing the Lord's command "to pray always," the notion that such prayer is liturgy or somehow special has undergone drastic rethinking. This theological problem is being treated here because for some people, clergy and religious especially, it may be a "hang-up" hindering them from a vital approach to group prayer in our day. It is the purpose of this section to show that, theologically, the Church has come around to saying that any gathering of Christians for prayer is liturgy, provided true orthodoxy is preserved, and that this notion is closest to the early Christian understanding and practice.

The Septuagint, the Greek translation of the Old Testament, came to use the word "liturgy" for the service of prayer and sacrifice rendered to the Lord.[8] Later on, in the New Testament writings, the word was used in reference to the sacrifice of Christ: "We have seen that he has been given a ministry *(leiturgia)* of a far higher order. . . ." (Heb 8:6).

A key text for our purposes occurs in Acts 13:1-2: "Now there were in the congregation at Antioch prophets and teachers: Barnabas, and Symeon who was called Niger, and Lucius of Cyrene, and Manaen, a close associate of Herod the tetrarch, and Saul. And as they worshiped the Lord and fasted. . . ." The word for worship here in Greek is *leiturgein,* and it is variously translated "ministered," "served" and "offering worship." E. Haenchen comments on this passage: "LXX [the Septuagint] uses *leiturgein* of the Temple service of the priests and Levites, *Didache* 15 [uses the word] of the *regular conduct of the Christian services.* Here the thought is of a gathering for communal prayer at which the circle of prophets and teachers is moved to a decision" (italics added).[9]

Though Luke's use of the term in Acts 13:2 stands

in contrast with the LXX, Jewish Christian circles of the time would not regard it as unprecedented or strange. Nevertheless, the verse demands special attention. For it is the first to attest a transfer of the important Old Testament cultic term to the purely spiritual Christian service of God, even though the reference be only to a small prayer fellowship of leading men.[10]

The verse indicates "movement toward a new Christian terminology . . . for a fellowship of prayer. . . ."[11]

In the course of time, the word became attached to only certain forms of group prayer, namely, the Eucharist, the sacraments and the Divine Office. In recent past theology, it would never have been acceptable to call other forms of prayer "liturgy" in the technical sense of the word.

The Church prolongs the priestly mission of Jesus Christ mainly by means of the sacred liturgy. She does this in the first place at the altar. . . . She does it next by means of the sacraments. . . . She does it finally by offering to God . . . the daily tribute of her prayer of praise" *(Mediator Dei,* No. 1).

From the text which follows this quotation, it is clear that "prayer of praise" refers only to the Divine Office.

While it was certainly true that anyone was free to pray the Office, certain people were deputed especially for this: "The Divine Office is the prayer of the Mystical Body of Jesus Christ, offered to God in the name and on behalf of all Christians, when recited by priests and other ministers of the Church and by religious deputed by the Church for this" *(Mediator Dei,* No. 122). There was an undeniable attitude created by this theological approach that, first, if you had not been deputed you were not really offering liturgical prayer, and, second, that, somehow, if you were deputed, your prayer was on a different (not to say better) level precisely for having been deputed.

Where did this notion of deputation come from, and what was its original meaning? In an article in *Concilium,* David Power, quoting B.D. Marliangeas, gives some clear and succinct answers. " 'The term "in the name of" was chosen to avoid "in the person of," and originated in a juridical context of no particular theological significance, simply as a way of explaining the obligation to recite the Divine Office imposed on these persons.' "[12]

It is difficult to argue with the fact that there was a practical mentality in the minds of priests and religious, arising from this juridical concept "of no particular theological significance," that the Divine Office was somehow even "better" prayer because deputed. It is important, then, to examine a little further, what makes prayer better theologically, and then see how the concept of liturgy begins to expand to include a much wider horizon.

The theological truth about prayer, namely, that the "charismatic call . . . and the answer to it, are of value to the Church,"[13] is the truth that needs to be appreciated. It is extremely important for everyone praying the Office (or Liturgy of the Hours) to realize that "without the grace, charity, and fervor of the person praying, this prayer is of no particular value."[14]

> Just as frequent reception of the sacraments does not automatically increase grace and give still more glory to God if not accompanied by a profounder dedication in faith, so too the Breviary is not "better" just because it is the "prayer of the Church" and is performed by "official mandate."[15]

It is all too easy to place the efficacy of our prayer on the fact of its being "official." What the charismatic renewal is doing, among other things, is recalling us to the essentials of prayer, those elements and attitudes without which our prayer cannot be acceptable to the Lord.

Then there is the refashioning of the concept of liturgy itself. In the documents of Vatican II there is a gradual pulling away from this restricted view of liturgy as "deputed prayer," although compromise statements are still in evidence. For example: "Therefore, when this wonderful song of praise is worthily rendered by priests and others who are deputed for this purpose. . . ." *(Constitution on the Liturgy,* No. 84). Such statements represent the theology of *Mediator Dei* and recent past approaches.

Further on we read: "They too perform the public prayer of the Church who, in virtue of their constitutions, recite any short office . . . provided it is duly approved" (No. 98). One could argue that the "circle of deputation" is simply being widened. That is certainly true, although the approach is different. The *content* which designates liturgy, i.e., any short office, is widened, and anyone who prays this is thereby "deputed."

The two notions are becoming looser. "And the laity too are encouraged to recite the Divine Office among themselves, either with priests, or among themselves, or even individually" (No. 100). It is theologically true to say, at this point in the development, that anyone praying any approved office is sharing in the official prayer of the Church. The "deputation" element has now been dissolved.

If it is clear that no formal deputation is any longer required since everyone is invited to pray the Liturgy of the Hours, are formal texts required, "approved texts," to constitute liturgy properly so called? We have already noted

Pope Paul's Apostolic Constitution, *Laudis Canticum*. He also says in that document that "the whole life of the faithful constitutes a *leiturgia* as it were. . . ."[16]

Although one might not be able to use such a text as a strict theological guideline, the attitude portrayed by it is indicative of the broadening of the meaning of liturgy to include more than approved texts. When one looks at the prayer of the Liturgy of the Hours, and then at various other kinds of prayer in the Church, it is theologically very difficult, if not impossible, to say why one form should be classified as liturgy and others not.

> To classify only the Divine Office as the prayer of the Church, and call everything else either public devotions or private prayer, seems arbitrary. The prayer of the Church incorporates a wide variety of realities; and each particular form is to be valued according to the measure of the fervor of the participants and the sacramental realization of the Church which it represents.[17]

The prayer of the Church, or the Church at prayer, admits of many degrees of intensity and sacramentalization. "Intensity" refers to faith, hope and love, and these are indispensable, and, it might be added, not capable of being measured or neatly classified.

The "sacramentalization" refers to the content of the prayers and songs, the way these are expressed and by whom, and the ceremonies and art forms connected with expressing worship. For example, all the bishops of the world praying the Liturgy of the Hours in St. Peter's together with the Holy Father achieve a high point of sacramentalization. Sacramentalization ought to lead to deeper intensity.

Sacramentalization in our case ought to express the nature of the Roman Catholic Church. To use certain readings, or recite certain prayers which do not reflect this nature reduces sacramentalization, and if the reduction is serious enough could cease to make that liturgy the prayer of the Church.

But can it any longer be denied that where Catholics come together in faith and love and use prayers and songs in perfect conformity with Church teaching, that this is not liturgy in every sense of the word? "Where two or three are gathered together . . ." receives once again its rightful place in theological thought.

Up to this point we have been concerned with certain aspects of the breviary reform and the reformulation of the theological notion of liturgy. Reform and renewal, however, are not the same thing. Renewal is the goal. Reform has to do with the outward structure; renewal is a much deeper matter of the Spirit at work in the hearts of men. Renewal is a matter of changed attitudes and ways of living. It is a matter of conversion of heart.

The present author believes that the charismatic renewal is one of the Spirit's instruments for prayer renewal in the Church today. At the present time, all over the world, literally thousands of prayer groups meet each week, and sometimes more often. If a person were skeptical about everything else in the charismatic renewal, he would certainly have to admit that this phenomenon of prayer meetings is in itself (as was mentioned above) a real moral miracle. There is truly a renewal of prayer taking place in the very heart of the Church.

What do these people do when they come together? They do exactly what historians of early Christianity say the early Christians did—they sing songs to the Lord, pray to him, recite the psalms, instruct one another, and share their lives in Christ. These are the same elements present in the Liturgy of the Word before the Eucharist, and in the Liturgy of the Hours, the only difference being that in these latter two, the elements are formalized and set in definite patterns. To state the difference in another way, in the prayer meetings these elements are free-flowing and more spontaneous—outpourings of the Spirit, charismatic.

This latter element—free and spontaneous outpourings of the Spirit—is the "missing element" needed to restore all Christian prayer to its original vigor and originality. The return of these free outpourings in prayer is the Spirit's distinctive contribution to the prayer renewal, a contribution that could never have been the outcome of reform or of a committee, no matter how well-intentioned. Through the charismatic renewal the Spirit is supplying the missing factor—charisms—for a fully mature prayer meeting. What needs to happen next is for the Church to officially incorporate these charismatic elements into her official prayer forms.

This is already happening through the inspired initiative of the Christian people themselves. For example, when people involved in the charismatic renewal came together for the 1972 conference at Notre Dame, charismatic elements were quite beautifully and spontaneously incorporated into the Liturgy of the Word before the Eucharist. It was the present author's personal vision come true of what a Christian prayer assembly should be. Everything was present and in order. There was intense devotion on the part of the people, charismatic manifestations, full sacramentalization through the presence of bishops, priests, scriptures and Eucharist. It would seem to be an ideal for the future to allow a place for charismatic elements in the celebration of every Eucharist.

With regard to the full restoration of the Liturgy of the Hours, several points may be worth noting. First, there is a place in the official revision of the Office for spontaneity, albeit a very small place. It occurs after the petitions. Those praying are invited to make spontaneous petitions, much in the same manner as at the Prayer of the Faithful at the Eucharist. Though the postconciliar commission probably did not envision this to be a spot for prolonged charismatic outpourings, nevertheless, the principle of and the need for spontaneous prayer is recognized and given a place. There is no theological reason why this could not be the place for charismatic prayer lasting ten minutes or an hour. Charismatic elements could be restored to the Liturgy of the Hours at this point.

It is not being suggested here that the Liturgy of the Hours in its Roman Catholic format should become the structure for the weekly prayer meeting which is completely unstructured most of the time. This would hardly happen, in any case. One of the providential thrusts of these weekly prayer meetings is ecumenical, and to use a specifically Roman Catholic format would be an unnecessary obstacle.

But in more homogeneous Catholic groups such as convents, rectories, apostolic societies in parishes, friends in the same neighborhood, in families, etc., the new revised Liturgy of the Hours does provide a quite simple and beautiful framework. Neither the framework nor the choice of songs or prayers or psalms need be rigidly adhered to. Only an overstrict view of "freedom in the Spirit" would look upon such a framework as restrictive. What prayer meetings often lack is a sense of praying with the Church. The use of a common yet fairly loose structure might provide that sense of praying with our brothers and sisters around the world, especially those united with us in the same communion. At the present time, prayer meetings could use an increased awareness of this ecclesial dimension.

The new Liturgy of the Hours could form a beautiful and simple format for daily family prayer. Already "charismatic families" are praying together daily. It is difficult to imagine a more perfect prayer renewal in the Church than this—families praying together.

Our modern way of life may preclude people from coming together daily, but there is no practical reason why families cannot do so. For our spiritual ancestors, the Jewish people, liturgy is properly a home phenomenon. For them the home is now the temple. The new Liturgy of the Hours as presented in the interim breviaries has the traditional, doctrinal and artistic elements to make family prayer, and group prayer in general, more sacramentally the prayer of the Church. The rest of the Christian life would then be well on its way to becoming a true *leiturgia*.

In an overall approach to group prayer, what we need is balance between spontaneity and format. Further, what is required is an ongoing methodology with regards to group prayer in the Church. Some elements of such a methodology would be as follows:

We must know our heritage, and seek the wisdom to distinguish the accidentals from the essentials. We must keep an eye on the newer, developing forms of prayer, not simply to endorse them uncritically, but to be able to recognize the finger of God when he tries to teach us new ways of praying.

Somehow too we must be good poets and artists as well as enthusiasts. Beauty and enthusiasm are not contradictory qualities, and yet the former often suffers or is nonexistent because of an overemphasis on spontaneity. Somehow there must be a place for both beauty of form and spontaneity, for freedom of expression and real artistic expression. Spontaneity is not opposed to planning and order and form. Spontaneity is opposed to an inability to listen to the movements of the Spirit.

There is much good material in our tradition that is still waiting to be used at present group prayer meetings. Perhaps our hesitation is due to legitimate fears. It is a lesson of history that in the tug-of-war between format/ structure and spontaneity, spontaneity has lost. Still, a balance must be sought so that the Lord may be praised with the best that we can offer him.

Another point of a methodology is that we must be honest with ourselves. We know when prayer is meaningful for us or not. When we judge that it is "not meaningful," we know that sometimes this is due to our own lack of effort in trying to understand and be receptive to either traditional or new approaches to prayer which may make demands on us. Sometimes personal effort is required to get "meaning" out of prayer forms.

But, on the other hand, we also sense sometimes in all sincerity, that the prayer form is bad, dull, repetitious, and really an obstacle to true prayer. We need the wisdom of discernment. With the help of the Spirit we must avoid both a superficial realism which demands excitement, novelty, and "in-depth meaning" every moment and at each new liturgy, and a blind adherence to the past which equates prayer with some sort of blind "suffering through" lifeless formulae. It is true that prayer is not easy for us in our condition of partial alienation from God, but neither ought it to be needlessly meaningless, tedious and painful.

One of my favorite sayings of Gandhi is: "There go my people, I am their leader, I must follow them." In this matter of prayer, the Church's duty is not confined to reforming official texts, necessary and helpful as this might be. The Church also has an obligation to follow the other leadings of the Spirit as he renews the prayer life of the Christian people in other ways. Wherever this Spirit is stirring and helping Christians to pray better, there the Church should be also, guiding, encouraging, and learning herself. As one of the Fathers of the Church said, "Every truth, no matter who speaks it, is of the Holy Spirit." So too, every true factor helping to renew prayer is of the Spirit, and the Church should be listening.

How should she be listening? The Church should be present at these weekly prayer meetings especially through her priests. The Church is most concerned about prayer, so much so that she spent a considerable amount of time discussing it at the Council. True Christian liturgy is taking place at these prayer meetings. Liturgy is at the heart of the Church's life, and the priest, as liturgist, should be present to guide and encourage. There should be some official move on the part of the Church to invite priests to these meetings. The people would be overjoyed at their presence.

A significant step in this regard appears in the recent document, *Spiritual Renewal of the American Priesthood,* issued by the United States Catholic Conference of Bishops. Among a list of "examples of the kind of interactional involvements which this document is strongly recommending to the bishops and priests of the United States as key to the spiritual renewal of the American priesthood," we read:

> Charismatic Renewal. Participation of priests in Pentecostal or charismatic prayer groups has not only

been previously recommended by a Committee of the American Bishops but also is particularly valuable in that it can lead a priest to a deeper experience of the presence of Christ, to a practical understanding of how the gifts of the Spirit mentioned by St. Paul (1 Cor 12) can work to build up a Christian community, and how these gifts can extend a priest's own ministry.[18]

"Preventative" is a household word these days. There is preventative medicine, preventative crime control, and so on. "Don't wait until you get sick, but take good care of yourself and prevent illness." Good advice! If, in years to come, aberrations become pronounced at prayer meetings, i.e., the scriptures are misinterpreted, prayers come out slightly heretical, prophecies begin to contradict the teachings of the Church, etc., if, I say, these things happen, the cause will not be enthusiasm or this "charisma stuff." Enthusiasm in the Spirit is a good thing; it just needs to be guided. Catholics, especially, seek and desire such guidance. But if aberrations occur and charisms are "squelched" again, one main reason will be because guidance from the clergy was not present when it should have been. "My flock is straying this way and that, on mountains and on high hills . . . no one bothers about them and no one looks after them" (Ez 34:6).

Chapter 9

...and Spirit Gives
Birth to Spirit

— Jn 3:6

One of the more fruitful areas of study which can help
to illuminate the charismatic renewal phenomenon is the
nature of human awareness, human consciousness. Many
exciting studies (e.g., *The Nature of Human Consciousness,*
ed. Robert Ornstein) have appeared recently which show
how the scientific enterprise has very much neglected the
intuitive, arational mode of man's consciousness as an
avenue to truth.

The same might be said about the pedagogy of the
Church. An extremely heavy burden was laid on the
rational powers of children. The truth was emphasized as
being "true concepts" about God and Christ. These truths
about God undoubtedly have their place in our relationship with the Lord. But there is another kind of knowing,
another avenue of truth which is inadequately described as
knowing God. Call it intuitive, arational, even mystical,
the name doesn't matter. We all know what is meant without trying to define it.

In the charismatic renewal, the gift of tongues is the
symbol of this approach to God. The fact that it *is* a gift
proves that such an arational approach to God is part of
our nature; and the fact that so many people pray for and

148

manifest this gift proves that it fulfills a need. This chapter is not about the gift of tongues, but about the wider area of consciousness of which it is a symbol. It explores the charismatic renewal as helping to foster an intuitive consciousness, and tries to situate that consciousness in our present historical context.

The universe is alive. This is one of the themes which the great mathematician and philosopher, A. N. Whitehead, tried to demonstrate in so many of his writings. There is a spontaneity and a creativeness at work in the world. What scientists thought were the ironclad laws of nature have turned out to be not so ironclad after all. Whether at the microcosmic or macrocosmic level, there are bursts of novelty which preclude any and all attempts on man's part to determine and program. Thank God for that! Otherwise man would surely devise some way of controlling the spontaneity in keeping with his preconceived notions of how things in the universe ought to run. Thus, throughout history, new geniuses have arisen, new religious figures, new currents of mind and heart which point man in the direction of his deepest reality.

These same unpredictable changes occur in people's lives in the form of religious conversions. In William James' classic, *The Varieties of Religious Experience,* he inquired as to the ultimate determining factor in religious conversion. How is it that ideas and attitudes once peripheral in a person's religious consciousness suddenly take a central place, and begin to form the habitual center of one's energies?

Now if you ask of psychology just *how* the excitement shifts in a man's mental system, and *why* aims that were peripheral become at a certain moment central, psychology has to reply that although she can give a general description of what happens, she is unable in a given case to account accurately for all the single forces at work. Our explanations . . . get so vague and general that one realizes all the more the intense individuality of the whole phenomenon.[1]

The religious person, the Christian, the theologian, would see the ultimate explanation for this change of heart in terms of grace, the breath of the Spirit who blows where he wills and when he wills. Only the Spirit of God is an adequate explanation for the renewal of man's heart; only he knows man's deepest needs and how to meet them.

For many people today the charismatic renewal is seen as a providential movement of the Spirit—and this from many different points of view.

It is seen as a renewal of prayer at a time when modern man is engulfed in a "death of God" complex and unable to believe anymore in a direct relationship with him. It is viewed as an ecumenical movement, the drawing together of all Christians on a basic level of fellowship and prayer in the Lord. It is seen as a revival movement: dead feelings, dead ideas, cold beliefs, are suddenly coming alive and turning red-hot. The Spirit is making dead bones come to life. These are so many ways of viewing a movement that was equally unpredictable a hundred years ago and which is unexplainable now in purely human terms.

The thrust of this chapter is to view the charismatic renewal from still another angle. It is meant to present the renewal as one of the factors helping to offset one of modern man's blind spots in regard to his view of reality. This defect has been variously called "single vision," "the myth of objective consciousness," and "scientific rationality." Too many people in our culture have bought whole-sale the notion that the scientific approach to reality is the only valid avenue to knowledge. It will be the purpose of this chapter to present some findings from a recent study in this area, and then to suggest that the expanded awareness brought about by the charismatic renewal is one of the factors helping to offset the myopia of single vision. But first, a few remarks about religious experience, which is one of the gateways to new horizons of consciousness.

The common denominator running through all the groups and peoples who claim participation in the charis-matic renewal is *religious experience.* It seems undeniable that one of the lessons the Spirit is trying to teach us today is the valid place of religious experience in the Christian life. Many characteristics of the spirituality of the renewal could be better understood if we understood better the effects of religious experience. At the present time it doesn't seem that we have an adequate theological approach to such experience.

George Montague, the present president of the Cath-olic Biblical Association, has recently stated that "the charismatic renewal has fostered a growth of spiritual con-sciousness unprecedented in the history of the U.S. Cath-olic Church."

This spiritual consciousness can be viewed from several angles. For example, people often speak of a "new birth in the Spirit," or they witness to the fact (or other people witness to the fact for them) that they are "new people." Some very enlightening studies have been made of this aspect of the charismatic experience.

Father Anthony Haglof, O.C.D., approaches it through the findings of analytical psychology: "Man, in other words, is so constituted that, on the one hand, he can be thrown out of the autonomous independence of his rational self-control by *inspiration,* which comes to him as a sudden and unpredictable force from outside of this sovereignty. . . ."[2] Haglof's article is highly recommended as an approach to the "newness" characteristics of the pentecostal experience.

More recently, Rosemary Haughton has used the framework of transactional analysis. She is talking about ecstatic states in general. She sees them as a "liberation of the 'original Child' and a release of the Child from Parent domination."[3] Those who have read Harris' book, *I'm OK, You're OK,* will remember that he had a section interpreting religious experience in the light of transactional analysis. One of his paragraphs especially bears citation here:

> What happens, then, in a religious experience? It is my opinion that religious experience may be a unique combination of Child (a feeling of intimacy) and Adult (a reflection on ultimacy) with the total exclusion of the Parent. I believe the total exclusion of the Parent is what is happening in *kenosis,* or self-emptying. This self-emptying is a common characteristic of all mystical experience. I believe that what is emptied is the Parent. I believe the Adult's function in the religious experience is to block out the Parent in order that the Natural Child may reawaken to its own worth and beauty as a part of God's creation.[4]

To rightly understand this passage, one would have to be familiar with Harris' definitions of Child, Parent and Adult. I find that in terms of his system of analysis, his explanation is an adequate one.

A second characteristic of experience, religious or otherwise, is that we come to know *not necessarily more but more deeply.* It's the difference between having a favorite movie star, and going out to lunch with him or her. It's the difference between knowing that "all men are mortal" as part of a logic course's syllogism, and being on one's deathbed. It's the difference between reading a book on the art of making lawn chairs, and actually making one.

Such changes in "knowing" are common to all of us and need no further elaboration. It explains, however, why people who have been recently "baptized in the Holy Spirit" speak of no longer merely knowing *about* Jesus, but of knowing *him.* Along the same lines, they testify that the words of scripture now seem to "leap out at them," whereas before they didn't seem to mean anything. The reason is that they've had an experience of the Author!

It would be possible to examine other dimensions of experience, apply them to religious experience, and then show how many characteristics of the renewal flow from experience. It can simply be noted here that many of the gifts of the Spirit are precisely in the realm of "knowledge" and different modes of consciousness (e.g., knowledge, wisdom, prophecy, teaching). It should also be noted that these gifts of the Spirit can grow and develop in Christians without any experience at all, but simply by the person's being faithful to the demands of the gospel in one's life. William James also pointed this out, and it is an important point to remember:

> The older medicine used to speak of two ways, *lysis* and *crisis,* one gradual, the other abrupt, in which one might recover from a bodily disease. In the spiritual realm there are also two ways, one gradual, the

other sudden, in which inner unification may occur.[5]

We know that an experience is morally neutral. It says nothing about a person's stance in the eyes of God. But an experience can rearrange one's center of consciousness, as stated above, and be the beginning of a whole new outlook on life. What the Spirit seems to be doing in the charismatic renewal is stepping up this unification through an experience process.

There is another effect of experience on man's knowing apparatus which is the specific topic of our concern here. We shall refer to Theodore Roszak's new book, *Where the Wasteland Ends,*[6] as our guide in this area.

The defect in Western man's psyche which we are concerned about, and which we believe is providentially being healed by the charismatic renewal, is best described negatively. It is a *narrowing of the sensibilities* for which modern man has opted as his definition of orthodox consciousness:

> My contention is that the universe of single vision, the orthodox consciousness in which most of us reside most of the time . . . is very cramped quarters, and by no means various and spacious enough to let us grow to full human stature.[7]

"What is to blame is the root assumption . . . that the transcendent aspirations of mankind . . . must be translated into purely secular equivalents . . . that culture must be wholly entrusted to the mindscape of scientific rationality." "One needs only ponder what people mean in our time when they counsel us to be 'realistic.' They mean . . . to regard the world as *nothing but* what the hard facts and quantitative abstractions of scientific objectivity make it out to be." "Science, for so long regarded as our single valid picture of the world, now emerges as . . . a school of consciousness, besides which alternative realities take their place."[8]

Roszak's book makes for exciting reading. He traces the rise and growth of this single vision in the founders of modern science, Bacon, Newton and Galileo, and in the Protestant reformers. He follows its development in the philosophies of Descartes and Locke. He has a marvelous chapter on the poet William Blake's sensitiveness to this truncated view of man, and how in the symbolism of his poetry he fought it the only way he knew how. Roszak then produces many examples from modern times to show how single vision has conquered. What follows is a very brief (and for that reason possibly misleading) account of the historical journey of single vision in the West as mapped out by Roszak. It is meant only to give the reader a bit of a taste of how we arrived at our present myopia.

Roszak claims that the Hebrew prophetic tradition's interpretation of idolatry was one-sided and incorrect. The prophets mocked those who bowed down before objects made by human hands (Is 43:13-18). Quoting Bevan: "It is hardly possible that anyone thought of the deity worshiped as simply the image he saw and nothing more." The ancient (pagan) mode of consciousness was more one of "participation": "the sense that there stands behind the phenomena, and on the other side of them from man, a *represented* . . . (Barfield)." The Jews withdrew radically from this participated consciousness. It passed over into early Christianity.

While extreme iconoclasts (e.g., Monophysites) have always existed, mainstream Christianity accepted visual imagery, but as *"nothing but* a statue, a mere symbol deprived of sacred personality." The magical mentality, which is basically sacramental perception, was confined within well-defined boundaries (the sacramental life of the Church). "Beyond lay demonology or pure fakery, the realm of bad magic." Such a stance did, however, save the believer from being inundated by superstition and crass charlatanry. But its final result was to cut man off from nature. Lactantius: ". . . the world does not produce man, nor is man a part of the world." Roszak comments: "This is a fateful ontology. Pressed to its ultimate conclusion, it yields a world in which nothing can be held sacred or companionable."

The Protestant Reformation brought iconoclast Christianity to a fever pitch. It ushers in a strange new stage of human consciousness. By harking back to the extreme prophetic consciousness of the Old Testament, the radical separation of sacred and profane, the Reformers carried the desacralization of nature to its annihilating extreme.

Idolatry became the psychic style of Bacon's "New Philosophy" 17th-century science. The real struggle between the Church and Galileo was due to the fact that the Christian psyche still retained Aristotelian concepts. His (Aristotle's) study of nature preserved . . . too much of the sense of nature alive . . . nature aglow with seductively sensuous qualities." Such remnants of "degraded pagan naturalism" had to be thrown off before true natural philosophy could arise. Roszak claims that Bacon's writings "contain the moral, aesthetic, and psychic raw material of the scientific world view."

Enter Newton. "With the Newtonian synthesis, Bacon's objectivized nature was at last achieved; the world picture was homogenized and qualitatively flattened. For the first time in the Western tradition, the universe became in the most objective sense of the word a 'universe': a cosmos uniform throughout its infinite extent, devoid of ethical nuance, of magic centers or charmed circles, of quintessential terrain. Henceforth, nature was seen to be spread out before the human observer like a value-neuter screen on which only the measurable behavior of things might be registered. And behind that screen, there was understood to be . . . nothing, no will, no animating purpose, no personality that might invite sensuous participation or answer the human desire to penetrate and commune."[9]

Perhaps enough has been cited from the historical angle to give the reader a sense of the function of the charismatic renewal in this situation. Roszak remarks that the "next revolution (will be) the struggle to liberate the visionary powers from the lesser reality in which they have been confined." "This book has had much to say that is severely critical of the scientific world view. . . . I am convinced that a hard critique of its psychology now has everything to do with restoring our cultural health." "Single vision and 'Newton's sleep,' where we dreamt that only matter and history are real. . . . This has been the bad, mad ontology of our culture, and it derives from the myth of objective consciousness. As long as that myth rules the mind, not even the most humanely intentioned among us will find any course to follow but roads that lead deeper into the wasteland."[10]

One of the keys to locked consciousness, one of the roads out of the wasteland which Roszak mentions and which is of special interest to us here, is *experience*. "Until we find our way once more to the *experience of transcendence* (italics mine), until we feel the life within us and the nature about us as sacred, there will seem to us no 'realistic' future other than more of the same: single vision and the artificial environment forever and ever, Amen." "It is the experience that must reopen those issues, not academic discourse. If there is to be a next politics, it will be a religious politics . . . vision born of transcendental knowledge."

How can such a vision be brought about? "Such a spiritual regeneration happens of its own mysterious accord or not at all. And of course it is happening. The signs of regeneration can be seen all about us in the heightened appetite for experience, the often indiscriminating passion to explore every forgotten reality of the self and nature."[11]

Curiously enough, Lewis Mumford, the great historian of technology and culture, points to a similar experience as a necessary factor if man is to turn from the madness of scientific rationality. His comment is all the more important as it comes at the very end of his massive study, *Pentagon of Power:*

> For its effective salvation, mankind will need to undergo something like a *spontaneous religious conversion* (italics mine): one that will replace the mechanical world picture with an organic world picture, and give to the human personality, as the highest known manifestation of life, the precedence it now gives to its machines and computers. Of only one thing we may be confident. If mankind is to escape its programmed self-extinction, the God who saves us will not descend from the machine: he will rise up again in the human soul.[12]

The present author believes that the charismatic renewal is providing one of the experiences of transcendence of which Roszak speaks. The regeneration which "happens of its own mysterious accord" is happening through the power of the Spirit of Jesus. It is undeniable that those who have had such a pentecostal experience have been opened up to believe in a much wider world than perhaps they ever believed in before. They are being opened to the reality of God, if this was absent. They are being opened to new ways of knowing through the gifts of prophecy, wisdom, knowledge and discernment. They are becoming more aware of the reality of good and malevolent spirits. They are beginning to see dreams as a possible way of God communicating with us (though we have still to develop anything approaching a theology of dreams).

Of course, I am not saying that only people who have had a charismatic experience are aware of or open to the world of spiritual realities (though I believe most people have had such experiences). What is being asserted is that for some people in our culture who have been conditioned to accept the scientific world view as the only correct criterion of the real, the charismatic experience is helping them overcome this single vision.

We are witnessing, as Roszak and others have pointed out, a hankering after experiences in many bizarre ways— drugs, satanism, witchcraft, heightened sense experiences of all kinds. Cannot these also help one to break out of single vision? Yes, they can, and probably do help people— break out of single vision, that is. But breaking out of single vision is only one small problem of the wholeness of life. We can have a "rhapsodic intellect" about harmful things. It was this insight which led the Church to restrict the vision of the faithful to only certain areas. The best tradition of the Church sees all of creation as sacramental.

She does teach, however, that it is dangerous to expose oneself to the spiritual world except in and through the Spirit of Jesus.

It would be unfortunate if the consciousness flowing from the charismatic experience did not flower into a true sacramental view of all of reality in Christ. St. Francis of Assisi's vision was not confined to the sacraments of the Church. He achieved such a communion with nature that sun and moon and stars were treated as his brothers and sisters. A kind of animism? Perhaps. But Francis also knew that not all spirits were his friends, and that not all ways of entering the spiritual world were good. No doubt many people who search for an "experience of the transcendent" are attempting to enter a more rarified world where their spirits can breathe. Perhaps their basic instinct is correct. The Christian would simply say—the Church would say—that in the Spirit of Christ we have access and entrance into this world. Jesus is the "Way In," and any other way can be misleading, or even dangerous.

Many young people who seek wider worlds haven't looked toward Christ as an entrance to this new life. It may be because they don't really know about him, or have no one to help them discover who he is. It may be too that some of them are more interested in mere experiences and not really in becoming better persons. A life of continually seeking experiences is not the answer to our needs, neither has Christ come to keep us on a religious-high trip of some kind. But Christ certainly wants to open us up to the spiritual world; he certainly wants to be our guide along the paths of spiritual experience.

In conclusion. The charismatic experience fits in well with many needs of modern man. Among other things, it equips him with new intuitive eyes with which to view the world. It can enable him to break out of the myth of objective consciousness. If modern man can open himself to this gift of God, he will become a participant in that "new politics." He will share in what Roszak calls the great adventure of our age. He will share in the true revolution of helping to bring to birth a wholeness in man's stance toward reality.

"I believe that we have arrived, after a long journey, at a historical vantage point from which we can at last see where the wasteland ends and where a culture of human wholeness begins."[13] The charismatic renewal is one of the experiences of transcendence for our times. It is that "spontaneous religious conversion" rising up from within the human soul. It is the merciful and gracious finger of God renewing our hearts as he promised. The full Christian tradition has never lost this wholeness in the face of reality. But it is a fact that a vast majority of people have. In the charismatic renewal, may we not be at a point in history where we can not only see where the wasteland ends, but where the wheat fields begin?

"Hearken to me, you who pursue deliverance, you who seek the Lord . . . For the Lord will comfort Zion, he will comfort all her *wastelands,* and will make her wilderness like Eden" (Is 51:1, 3).

Epilogue

Sometimes it is only at the conclusion of writing a book—after you yourself as an author have read it over a few times—that you finally come to really appreciate the underlying theme or themes which prompted the writing of it in the first place. Being now in that position, I see that the theme, the underlying presupposition, which has been guiding my efforts and the choice of material is *balance*. This book has been a plea for balance with regard to the charismatic renewal in the Church.

Someone asked John Courtney Murray once whether he was a liberal or a conservative. With a disarming seriousness he answered, "My dear fellow, I am in the extreme center!" The extreme center. A paradoxical phrase, easily confused in theory and practice with mediocrity and with walking an overprudent line in between positions neither of which are all too exciting.

Yet there is a romance about the extreme center. It is akin to what Chesterton means by the romance of orthodoxy. There are so many aspects of our faith which are true all at the same time; if you overemphasize any one of them, somehow the others diminish, and the one emphasized becomes in a way untrue. It's like standing in the middle of forces coming at you from all directions. You seem to be standing still—and you are—but you are charged with a terrific amount of energy at the swirling, vibrant center.

Using the incomparable prose and genius of the late Monsignor Ronald Knox, I would like to try and sum up the main theme of this book. Knox's *Enthusiasm*[1] is one of the best books I have ever read. Of late, it has been used, more often than not, as an arsenal of lessons from history to point out the *dangers* of the charismatic renewal. This is only natural as the book deals with the aberrations of religious enthusiasm. I often wished that Monsignor Knox had written a companion volume dealing with enthusiasts who stayed *in* the Church. As it is, all his genius and mastery of the English language were brought to bear more on the aberrations of enthusiasm than on its merits.

But if one reads the book sympathetically, one will see the many sections in which he noted the virtues of enthusiasm also. By using some selections from his book, I will try to briefly sum up what I have been attempting to say throughout this book.

"Let us note, from the first, that traditional Christianity is a balance of doctrine, and not merely of doctrines but of emphases. You must not exaggerate in either direction, or the balance is disturbed."

Our thinking tends to follow our feelings. It works the other way too, of course, but more unconscious is the process of evolving theories to follow or justify how we feel. When one has been filled with the charismatic experience, care must be observed that such enthusiasm does not unduly change doctrine.

"An excellent thing to abandon yourself, without reserve, into God's hands; if your own rhetoric leads you into fantastic expressions of the idea, there is no great harm done. But, teach on principle that it is an infidelity to wonder whether you are saved or lost, and you have overweighted your whole devotional structure; you have ruled out a whole type of religious self-expression.

"Conversely, it is a holy thing to trust in the redeeming merits of Christ. But, put it about that such confidence is the indispensable sign of being in God's favor, that, unless and until he is experimentally aware of it, a man is lost, and the balance has been disturbed at the opposite end; you have condemned one type of religious mind to despair."

Cannot religious experience have a positive effect on our own understanding of doctrine? Certainly, and I think the charismatic renewal has shown exactly what that effect can be.

The "baptism in the Holy Spirit" helps people to know their faith "from the center outward," as it were. It is no longer (if it was in the past) an ensemble of unconnected truths and notions lacking unity. That's the key word: unity. The charismatic experience has helped people to unify their faith. Life and thought are now more fused. The love of God, mediated to them through Jesus and poured out by the gift of the Spirit, has become central in their faith consciousness. Not to somehow realize this truth is somehow not to know what being a Christian is.

Because an experience is precisely so unifying, so centering, there is a tendency—doctrinally, devotionally and ecclesiastically—to disregard or be impatient with what might come to appear as "peripheral" matters. One wishes only to be concerned with the "heart of the matter" and has little or no interest—little or no patience—with other things.

The enthusiasm of the Spirit, if combined with only half-truths about man, can produce a strange kind of human being. The American psyche is still permeated with some strange notions about man. Many of the early aberrations in Christianity were due to the fact that people who had no Jewish background or tradition were coming to believe in Jesus. Rich Semitic and Hebrew concepts were misunderstood or distorted. To mention one of many possible examples, "flesh" and "spirit" became "body" and "soul"; for many Christians matter became evil. The Jewish sense of the wholeness of life, the goodness of creation, had been lost.

Similarly, enthusiasm in the Spirit can simply charge half-truths about man with new vigor. If one has a strict Anglo-Saxon concept of law, a charismatic experience can turn one into a new type of legalist. If one has a puritan attitude toward the things of creation, enthusiasm can reinforce the tendency to depreciate creation as a means of rising to the Creator.

On the positive side, the charismatic experience has helped many people to rediscover the joy of the Christian life. They have come to realize that it isn't irreverent to really be happy and expressive at worship. A new sense of oneness with their brothers and sisters in Christ has freed them to show affection by touch, embrace and the holy kiss.

A certain dissatisfaction with externals can arise from the charismatic experience and manifest itself in particular attitudes toward worship. "It involves a new approach to religion; hitherto this has been a matter of outward forms and ordinances, now it is a matter of the heart. Sacraments are not necessarily dispensed with; but the emphasis lies on a direct personal access to the Author of our salvation with little of intellectual background or of liturgical expression. The appeal of art and music, hitherto conceived as a ladder which carried human thought upwards, is frowned upon as a barrier which interferes with the simplicity of true heart-worship."

The charismatic renewal has brought a stupendous realization to the forefront of the Church's religious consciousness: If one does not pray from the heart, one is not praying at all! It is trying to restore one of the missing elements of the Christian worship service: spontaneity. Deep in our hearts we know that the real challenge is some harmonious blending of spontaneity and form, a blending which would be beautiful without being lifeless, and full of life without being aesthetically shoddy.

As Knox points out to us, what is really at stake are various theologies of grace. "Our traditional doctrine is that grace perfects nature, elevates it to a higher pitch, so that it can bear its part in the music of eternity, but leaves it nature still. The assumption of the enthusiast is bolder and simpler: for him, grace has destroyed nature, and replaced it." Enthusiasm must be careful of wreaking havoc with nature; others must beware of settling for a nature unredeemed.

I mentioned in Chapter 9 that the charismatic experience is an arational experience. One comes to "know God" in an intuitive way. This is good, and one of the ways we come to know God. Knox has much to say about the attempt to make this the *only* way.

"Especially, he (the enthusiast) decries the use of human reason as a guide to any sort of religious truth. A direct indication of the Divine will is communicated to him at every turn, if only we will consent to abandon the 'arm of flesh'—Man's miserable intellect, fatally obscured by the Fall. That God speaks to us through the intellect is a notion which he may accept on paper, but fears, in practice, to apply.

"Generally characteristic . . . is a distrust of our human thought-processes. In matters of abstract theology, the discipline of the intellect is replaced by a blind act of faith. In matters of practical deliberation, some sentiment of inner conviction, or some external 'sign' indicative of the Divine will, claims the priority over all consideration of common prudence."

Modern studies on the functions of the brain are revealing to us that rational/logical thinking and intuitive apprehension are the two ways by which our minds reach out to know the reality around us. The charismatic experience is doing much to open up man's intuitive powers and to be sensitive to all the arational ways by which the Holy Spirit tries to guide and inspire us. For all that, we dare not forget that "our mental powers are also from God; to write these off as hopelessly corrupted by the Fall is an extravagance quite unwarranted by Christian tradition."

These quotes from Knox are not meant to be characterizations of attitudes of the present charismatic renewal. I believe that my book indicates how healthy, generally, I think the charismatic renewal is at the present time. However, Knox does masterfully describe what may be the attitudes of some, and what are always potential dangers.

In this last and final quote, he reveals the dangers of both sides in regard to structure and charism. I believe it sums up better than anything else both his own attitude and mine toward the phenomenon of enthusiasm in the Church.

"More than all the other Christianities, the Catholic Church is institutional. (It is) too easily concluded that she is thereby incapacitated from all spiritual initiative, David in Saul's armour; history makes short work of the conclusion. New things as well as old she keeps in her treasure house: you will find current coin there, not only obsolete doubloons.

"But there is danger in her position nonetheless; where wealth abounds, it is easy to mistake shadow for substance; the fires of spirituality may burn low, and we go on unconscious, dazzled by the glare of tinsel suns. How nearly we thought we could do without St. Francis, without St. Ignatius! Men will not live without vision; that moral we do well to carry away with us from contemplating, in so many strange forms, the record of the visionaries. If we are content with the humdrum, the second-best, the hand-over-hand, it will not be forgiven us."

NOTES

Chapter 1

1. Gregory Baum, *Man Becoming*, p. 15.
2. Paul Tillich, *The Courage to Be*, p. 2.
3. *Ibid.*, p. 47.
4. Rudolf Bultmann, *Jesus Christ and Mythology*, p. 57.
5. *Ibid.*, p. 58.
6. *Ibid.*, pp. 40-41.
7. Tillich, *op. cit.*, p. 160.
8. *Ibid.*, p. 9.
9. A. N. Whitehead, *Adventures of Ideas*, p. 279.
10. *Ibid.*, p. 258.
11. *Ibid.*
12. *Op. cit.*, p. 185.
13. John B. Cobb, Jr., *A Christian Natural Theology*, pp. 217-218.

Chapter 2

1. Vincent Taylor, *The Doctrine of the Holy Spirit*, p. 41. Quoted by C. K. Barrett, *The Gospel and the Holy Spirit Tradition*, p. 1.

Chapter 3

1. Ernest S. Williams, *Systematic Theology,* Vol. III, pp. 39-61. This is one of the few systematic theologies written by classical Pentecostals. The author was for 20 years General Superintendent of the General Council of the Assemblies of God.

2. Kilian McDonnell, O.S.B., and Arnold Bittlinger, *The Baptism in the Holy Spirit as an Ecumenical Problem,* pp. 47-48.

3. A. H. Couratin, "Liturgy," *The Pelican Guide to Modern Theology,* ed. R. P. C. Hanson, Vol. 2, p. 170.

4. James D. G. Dunn, *Baptism in the Holy Spirit,* Vol. 15: *Studies in Biblical Theology,* p. 4.

5. *Ibid.,* pp. 224-226.

6. Couratin, *op. cit.,* p. 161.

7. *Ibid.,* p. 199.

8. Couratin, *op. cit.,* p. 200.

9. *Ibid.,* p. 199.

10. *Ibid.,* p. 205-206.

11. McDonnell, *op. cit.,* pp. 44-46.

12. Kevin Ranaghan, "The Problem of Re-Baptism" (Mimeograph, Ann Arbor, Mich.) p. 1.

13. Donald L. Gelpi, "Understanding 'Spirit Baptism,'" *America* (May 16, 1970) p. 520.

14. Stephen B. Clark, "Confirmation and the Baptism of the Holy Spirit" (Pecos, New Mexico, Dove Publications, 1969) p. 15.

15. Kilian McDonnell, "Holy Spirit and Pentecostalism," *Commonweal* (November 8, 1968) p. 198.

16. Dunn, *op. cit.,* p. 225.

17. C. K. Barrett, *The Holy Spirit and the Gospel Tradition,* p. 1.

18. Vincent Taylor, *The Doctrine of the Holy Spirit,* p. 41. Quoted by Barrett, p. 1.

19. Francis A. Sullivan, S.J., "The Pentecostal Movement," *Gregorianum,* Vol. 53, 1972, p. 250.

20. Simon Tugwell, O.P., "He Will Baptize You With the Holy Spirit," *New Blackfriars* (June, 1971) pp. 270-271.

21. Sullivan, *op. cit.,* p. 250-251.

22. Williams, *op. cit.,* p. 39.

23. *Ibid.,* p. 41.

24. Dunn, *op. cit.,* p. 226.

25. Tugwell, *op. cit.,* p. 271.

26. "Transcript of Discussion on Pentecostalism," Eighth National Secretariat Meeting, October, 1969. Mimeograph.

27. Sullivan, *op. cit.,* p. 250.

28. Tugwell, *op. cit.,* p. 271.

Chapter 4

1. Edward O'Connor, *The Pentecostal Movement in the Catholic Church,* p. 264.

2. Derek Prince, *New Wine* (March, April, May).

3. *Ibid.,* April.

4. *Theological Dictionary of the New Testament,* Vol. VI, p. 853.

5. Donald Gelpi, *Pentecostalism: A Theological Viewpoint,* pp. 227-228.

6. Gunther Bornkamm, *Early Christian Experience,* p. 30.

7. *Op. cit.,* p. 220.

8. Hans Kung, *The Church,* pp. 196-198.

9. *Op. cit.,* p. 234.

10. Hans Von Campenhausen, *Ecclesiastical Authority and Spiritual Power in the Church of the First Three Centuries,* p. 263.

Chapter 5

1. Leon-Joseph Cardinal Suenens, *Coresponsibility in the Church* (New York: Herder and Herder, 1968) p. 30.

2. Hans Von Campenhausen, *Ecclesiastical Authority and Spiritual Power in the Church of the First Three Centuries* (Stanford, California: Stanford University Press, 1969).

3. Walter Bauer, *Orthodoxy and Heresy in Earliest Christianity* (Philadelphia: Fortress Press, 1971).

4. Von Campenhausen, 301.

5. *Ibid.*

6. *Ibid.,* 52.

7. *Ibid.,* 53.

8. *Ibid.,* 59.

9. *Ibid.,* 60.

10. *Ibid.*

11. *Ibid.,* 58.

12. *Ibid.*

13. *Ibid.*

14. *Ibid.,* 63.

15. *Ibid.,* 70.

16. *Ibid.,* 149.

17. *Ibid.,* 150.

18. *Ibid.,* 151.

19. *Ibid.*

20. *Ibid.,* 34.

21. *Ibid.,* 79.

22. *Ibid.,* 117.

23. *Process and Reality* (Free Press: New York, 1969) pp. 399-400.

Chapter 6

1. Rudolf Bultmann and Five Critics, *Kerygma and Myth,* p. 5.

2. Rudolf Bultmann, *Jesus Christ and Mythology,* pp. 36-37.

3. *Ibid.,* p. 51.

4. *Ibid.,* p. 15.

5. *Ibid.,* p. 16.

6. *Ibid.,* pp. 16-17.

7. *Kerygma*, pp. 10-11.

8. *Mythology*, p. 45.

9. *Ibid.*, p. 18.

10. *Kerygma*, p. 9.

11. *Mythology*, p. 46.

12. *Ibid.*, p. 46.

13. *Ibid.*, p. 14.

14. *Ibid.*, p. 52.

15. William Nicholls, *The Pelican Guide to Modern Theology,* Vol. 1: Systematic and Philosophical Theology, p. 165.

16. *Mythology*, p. 52.

17. For an amazing account of how a modern-day minister of the gospel became involved in the ministry of deliverance of evil spirits, cf. Don Basham's *Deliver Us from Evil* (Washington Depot, Connecticut: Chosen Books, 1972).

18. Raymond E. Brown, "Virginal Conception of Jesus," *Theological Studies,* Vol. 33 (March, 1972), p. 33. Father Brown's article has received such bad coverage in the press that we'd like to include here his own footnote (91) to the passage quoted in the present text:

> "In particular, as a Roman Catholic whose biblical studies have led him to appreciate all the more the importance of a teaching Church, I cannot resolve the problem [i.e., of the Virgin Birth] independently of the question of authority raised in my first section. I am not afraid that an honest discussion of the virginal conception will lead to a traumatic choice between fidelity to modern exegesis and fidelity to a teaching Church, provided that both the bible and tradition are subjected to intelligent historical criticism to find out exactly what was meant and the degree to which it was affirmed. Inevitably, however, openness to discussion will be misrepresented as denial of tradition." *Ibid.*, p. 33.

19. *Mythology*, p. 34.

20. Gregory Baum, *Man Becoming,* pp. 101-102.

21. *Mythology*, p. 43.

22. Nicholls, *op. cit.,* p. 185.

Chapter 7

1. *The National Catholic Reporter,* "Seeds of Unity Are Found in the Charismatic Renewal" (Jan. 19, 1973) p. 9.

2. *Reporter, op. cit.,* p. 5.

Chapter 8

1. Hans Kung, *The Living Church,* pp. 224-25.

2. Samuel Sandmel, *The First Christian Centuries in Judaism and Christianity,* pp. 78-79.

3. George Foote Moore, *Judaism in the First Centuries of the Christian Era,* Vol. 1, p. 296.

4. Adolph Harnack, *The History of Dogma,* Vol. 1, p. 332.

5. *Ibid.,* p. 53. The whole question of the factors which determined the suppression of charismatic elements in the early Church is rather unexplored. Montanism, and the reaction it caused, was a large factor, as has been noted.

6. *The Liturgy of the Hours* (Australia and London: Dwyer and Chapman, 1971), p. 11.

7. Quoted by Giles H. Pater, "The Parish Priest as Leader of Christian Prayer," *Worship,* Vol. 46, No. 4 (April, 1972), p. 224.

8. Gerhard Kittel (ed.), *Theological Dictionary of the Bible,* Vol. IV, pp. 227-28.

9. Ernst Haenchen, *The Acts of the Apostles,* p. 396.

10. Kittel, *op cit.,* p. 227.

11. *Ibid.,* p. 228.

12. Vol. 52: *Prayer and Community,* p. 101.

13. *Ibid.*

14. *Ibid.*

15. A. Haussling, art. "Breviary," in *Sacramentum Mundi* I, p. 238. Quoted by Power, *op. cit.,* p. 101.

16. Pater, *op. cit.,* p. 224.

17. Power, *op. cit.*, p. 100.

18. United States Catholic Conference (Publications Office, 1973), p. 68.

Chapter 9

1. (New York: Mentor Books, 1958), p. 162.

2. "Psychology and the Pentecostal Experience," *Spiritual Life,* Vol. 17, No. 1 (Spring, 1971), p. 203.

3. "Unless You Become as Little Children," *New Blackfriars,* (Nov.-Dec., 1973), p. 302.

4. (New York: Avon Books, 1967), p. 267.

5. James, p. 152.

6. (Garden City, N.Y.: Anchor Books, 1973).

7. *Ibid.,* p. 71.

8. *Ibid.,* pp. 71, 124, 159.

9. *Ibid.,* pp. 101-199, *passim.*

10. *Ibid.,* pp. xxii, 371, 422.

11. *Ibid.,* pp. 420-422.

12. (New York: Harcourt Brace Jovanovich, Inc.), p. 413.

13. Roszak, p. xvii.

Epilogue

1. (Oxford University Press, 1950). All quotations in this epilogue are from this book, 1-3; 580-591, *passim.*

ACKNOWLEDGMENTS

Grateful acknowledgment is made to the following periodicals for permission to use materials:

"Courage and Adventure in the Act of Conversion," from *Spiritual Life,* Summer, 1972.

"Baptism in the Holy Spirit," from *Cross and Crown,* Vol. XXV, No. 2, June, 1973.

"The Rebirth of Group Prayer," from *Cross and Crown,* Vol. XXV, No. 4, December, 1973.

"Bultmann and the Charismatic Renewal," from *Cross and Crown,* Vol. XXVI, No. 2, June, 1974.

"Is the Charismatic Renewal a New Montanism?" from *Homiletic and Pastoral Review,* Vol. LXXIII, No. 3, December, 1972.

"Office and Charisma," from *The American Ecclesiastical Review,* Vol. 167, No. 4, April, 1973.

"Where the Wheatfields Begin," from *The Priest* with permission of the Publisher. Copyright 1975 by Our Sunday Visitor, Inc., Huntington, Indiana.

"It Is Clear That There Are Serious Differences Among You," from *Review for Religious,* September, 1973.

"The Holy Spirit in the New Testament," *St. Anthony's Messenger,* February, 1975.